MW01244892

Foreword

It sure seemed much longer.

I worked at the Philadelphia Daily News for ten years, from 1998 to 2008. While it is impossible to distill my career into a number of stories, the ten proceeding articles went a long way towards defining my tenure at the paper.

I first came to the paper through a "Minorities in Journalism" job fair, one in which the editors of several Pennsylvania-based newspapers attended, many with the directive to hire a number of the qualified applicants.

After being summarily dismissed by the editors of the Pittsburgh Post- Gazette, I literally begged both the editor and Director of Human Resources of the Philadelphia Daily News to hire me in any capacity, and that all I needed was a foot in the door. I guess they either admired or grew tired of my persistence, and they instructed me to call the paper once I got back to Philly and set things up.

I was initially hired as a part-time clerk, which basically meant doing the grunt work and handling some of the more unpleasant issues that pop up in a newsroom. Still, I came there to write, and although I let everyone know it, the opportunities to write would be scarce.

In fact, I was told just that, not once, but twice, by two different editors. I will never forget approaching former City Desk Editor Yvonne Dennis and the Assistant Features Editor inquiring about my chances to write, and both telling me that I would never write for the paper.

Ten years later, I can say with great pleasure that not only did I become a journalist, I also won numerous awards, including recognition from the National Association of Black Journalists.

So in no small way, these are the stories that made me the writer I am today; I hope when you read these stories, you will see what I have seen, and felt what I have felt during my years of covering the streets of Philadelphia. Many of these stories are heart breaking; all were interesting and caused me a great deal of introspection. You will also notice the prevalence of newsroom politics, and what happens when a reporter bumps up against the old-school industry hierarchy that has felled a number of young and veteran reporters alike.

The stories were one thing; this is my truthful, sometimes explicit recollection of the stories behind the stories. In many ways, it is only fitting that this work has its gritty and profane elements, for it mirrors what I often confronted on a daily basis.

I hope you enjoy these stories; and if you were to come away with a better understanding of Philadelphia, journalism and The Philadelphia Daily News, we will all be the better for it.

-Dame, November 2011

-First Revision, November 2020

SOUL IN INK:

The Memoirs of a Journalist

INDEX

*Paul Rusesabagina Speaks at Free Library of Philadelphia.

*Ex-Offenders Panel (the Story of Kalief Tucker).

*The Murder of Fassara Kouyate.

*Staying Alive (the Story of Dr. Amy Goldberg).

CHAPTER ONE:

Interview with Nation of Islam Leader Minister Louis Farrakhan, RE: Millions More March, October 2005.

I have always looked at my interview of Nation of Islam leader Minister Louis Farrakhan as one of the two high-water marks of my career. And it had less to do with reporting skills directly, but much more to do with the ability to convince Farrakhan's handlers that I was the one journalist that could be trusted to deliver his message, unfiltered, to the masses.

And trust he did, but gaining said trust proved to be a case study in perseverance and the fortunes of having a solid reputation as a stand-up black journalist who would rather not write a story at all than to have it come out off- beat and it cause more harm than good.

It started simply enough. At first, the local chapters of the Millions More Movement contacted the paper to do a writeup on the local preparations for the Millions More March, which served as the tenth year anniversary of the Million Man March.

Michael Days, the Editor-In-Chief who had recently took over for the departed Zack Stalberg, and Kurt Heine, who was City Desk Editor at the time, assigned me as the exclusive reporter to cover every aspect of the event and to come up with several pieces revolving around it: preparations, intentions and local logistics.

A big assignment, sure, but one I was more than capable of handling.

By that time, I had cultivated a reputation in the newsroom as one of the go-to reporters to cover black issues and developments.

I didn't mind too much at the stereotypical assignments, since it was basically the type of coverage I wanted to do in the first place. But more on that later.

Also at the time, Farrakhan was and remained a polarizing figure who in my estimation, tried to bridge lots of water and form alliances with groups that the average person would think the Nation of Islam would have nothing to do with.

I followed my usual routine when I approached this story, but I had a little more background than the average reporter, because ten years prior, I was an Executive Board Member of La Salle University's African American Student League, and we helped spearhead neighborhood interest and chartered a bus to take the inspired men to the nation's capital to participate in the march.

The female members of the board and other supporters withstood the bone-chilling weather and stood side-by-side with us in the brisk pre-dawn wind as we waited to board the bus, sending us off with homemade food. It was quite the event; so naturally, I already knew from which angles to approach the story and did so with zest.

Doing the background reporting for this story was rather easy, because I knew right where to look and exactly who to talk to.

The hard part was convincing Farrakhan's handlers to give me ten minutes or so on the phone with the enigmatic and controversial minister.

It proved to be a daunting task.

At the time and to my understanding, that was the very first full-length print interview Farrakhan has ever done with a daily, mainstream (I.E. 'white') newspaper. And considering that the Philadelphia Daily News didn't exactly enjoy the best of relationships with its African-American readership, I was doubtful that Farrakhan would actually grant the interview.

But reputation goes a long way, and after a series of phones calls and checks with numerous third-party individuals who knew of me and my work, I found myself on the phone with Farrakhan, both amazed and astounded that I was actually about to talk with someone of such magnitude.

I have spoken with several prominent figures in all realms of society, including luminaries such as former Secretary of State Madeleine Albright, but I must admit, this was the first and only time where I thought of an interview as a once-in-alifetime, career-defining moment.

And for the first time, I felt in over my head.

One can say what they will about Farrakhan, but most people can agree that he has been one of the most provocative speakers and leaders of the past half-century.

And after being patched through a few times and dealing with a number of live connectors (no doubt for security reasons and to make sure the line was secure), Farrakhan greeted me with words I will never forget. "Good afternoon, brother."

Sure, it may seem to be three simple words when one reads it, but Farrakhan's tone instantly eased my nerves. I guess I, too, fell into the trap of believing the negative hype and what everyone has read about the man, because I braced myself for Farrakhan to be very abrasive and confrontational with me; after all, I was a member of the mainstream media – white media.

And I must be some sort of so-called 'Uncle Tom' to be working in that field, or worst, some type of race traitor. After all, I had been accused of that and much worse during my Daily News tenure.

And no matter my chops and skills, I wasn't ready to have a battle of wits with the minister.

Apprehension aside, I hastily told Farrakhan what an honor it was for me to be speaking with him, and that I seen him in person during a speech in Philly years ago, while I assured him that his quotes would run as intended.

This wasn't above and beyond any promise any journalist makes to any subject; in fact, any good journalist will run quotes as stated, regardless. I even went above that threshold, often giving the subjects a chance to collect their thoughts and to be certain that what was just said was the intended onrecord quote they wanted printed in the paper.

This does go against a certain dogma of news reporting, but when it comes to the science of actual journalism, it pays to give people a chance to say exactly what they mean.

There's usually an agenda (besides poor writing and editing) when quotes appear misconstrued in the paper. It's just bad business. Still, in some unexplainable way, it felt good to make – and ultimately keep – a promise to Minister Farrakhan – not that the minister needed that type of easy out.

As Farrakhan talked about the public marches he helped initiate and the piggybacking marches that sprung up following 1995, I felt that Farrakhan was ministering directly to me. Not only that, I could immediately tell that he cared immensely not only for the black people of America, but for society as a whole. `That might be hard to believe, given Farrakhan's more explosive statements, but trust me, I could feel his sentiment through his words. Maybe that was his time- honed ministerial style or perhaps he could sense my star-struck nature, but I was a believer in a matter of minutes.

About the march itself, Farrakhan was upbeat about the advances made, and believed that he realize his goal of reaching as many folks as possible.

"I believe it's gradually picking up momentum. We're in 400 cities in America, forming local organizing committees composed of all the civil-rights organizations, the youths, nationalists and pan-Africanists, those that have been on the front line of reparations.

"We have a very broad cross-section of black thought and black life coming aboard to help mobilize. Not just for the commemoration, but mobilized to create a movement that will put on our shoulders the job to repair that which was done to us: 350 years of slavery and 150 years of Jim Crow injustice."

No doubt about it, Farrakhan has an ability to push certain buttons within society and force discussion on issues that, by and large, people are uncomfortable with; slavery, racism and reparations are but three.

As someone who was a Farrakhan sympathizer (if not outright Nation of Islam member) during my college years, I already formed an opinion that he may have been misguided in some of his statements and that the media has portrayed him in a most unfavorable light, but I have always believed that he had the best interests of society at heart.

After all, he wasn't calling for genocidal warfare or claiming the Holocaust never happened. That's not to say that Farrakhan hasn't been wrong or caught up in controversy; I just didn't feel that sort of heat from him during our conversation.

I asked Farrakhan if African-American people, as whole, were better off now than they were ten years before, during the first march. His answer was startling.

"To be very honest, when the enemies of our rise saw the magnificence of the Million Man March, they fought against what they saw. Ten years later, although we have more public officials and more millionaires and billionaires, the masses of our people are in a worse condition today than we have ever been.

The job situation is horrendous, with black men unemployed, and they are not joining the armed forces. Then, the alternative for young black men becomes, do you get involved with crime, sell drugs or gang-bang? Youths are filling the prisons, and the murder rate is totally unacceptable."

That was deep.

To me, it seemed that Farrakhan was pained to come to that conclusion, and it was telling to hear a man who has devoted his entire life to the rise and equality of black people make such an assessment.

Farrakhan pointed to education and economics as two of the main factors contributing to his theory.

"We need a movement to organize the best and brightest of our people. That's one of the agendas for the Millions More Movement. Spiritual and moral development, and gathering our educational giants to create a new educational paradigm.

We need organized bankers to look at the $350 billion (the estimated annual income of African-Americans) that comes through our hands, and how we can attract this money back to our community. We need to create jobs and give our economy an opportunity. We have a lot to do. The government is not going to do it for us, so we must pool our resources."

Midway through our conversation, I asked Farrakhan if he thought that the proliferation of marches somehow dampened the message of the historic mass- demonstrations he helped create.

Where I thought he would have had a problem with it, Farrakhan, instead, welcomed the other marches and organizers, saying that they could all possibly work together.

One can certainly argue that the Million Man March spawned the latest era of organized mass rallies and protests.

"The Qur'an says to the Muslims, 'Bind with one another in every good work.' We are a people that saw the Million Man March, and the women were impressed, and thus came the Million Woman and Million Youth marches.

Now, we're all together to put forth the Millions More Movement, creating a movement for political and economical power. Two million men, two million women, hundreds of thousands of youths and workers, all coming together to create this movement.

Most of our young black millionaires do what they can to give back to the community, but it's never enough," Farrakhan continued.

Williams

"This is why there must be a program for
economic development that our black
millionaires can invest in that would bring a
return to the community and a return to them.
Our mosques do it, Jay-Z and 50 Cent and
others—they are all doing it.

But if we set out a program, for instance,
where we need a hundred million acres of
land to provide for our people, we need to
pull our money together and buy it, so we can
produce what we consume."

For a split-second, I felt the urge to
challenge Farrakhan's assessment that Jay-Z
and 50 Cent are giving back to their
respective communities. But in that same
amount of time, there was no way I was
going to stop the minister in the middle of a
priceless interview just to argue the semantics
and definitions of "giving back."

Journalists are trained that, when dealing
with a controversial subject or a touchy topic,
to ask the hard questions last and ask the

more general questions first. That way, if the subject becomes angered or hangs up on you, you will have already obtained the background of the story.

And usually, if a reporter established a friendly, or at least a non-hostile rapport with the subject, it'll make asking those tougher questions easier.

With that in mind, my last question to Farrakhan was about his many distracters, and how he copes with the level of vitriol he has and continues to face. M u c h t o m y surprise, Farrakhan was much more diplomatic than I thought he would be. Or even should be.

"Whenever there is something of value, God always permits opposition. It's that opposition that attracts the will and strength to move forward," Farrakhan said. "The opposition is all right; it will never stop us from doing good, but it will inspire us to do more."

And with that, my interview with Minister Louis Farrakhan had concluded, but not before he said a few more words that I will also never forget.

"Brother, I must now go. But I want to tell you

that it has been my pleasure talking with you, and I hope you remain healthy and strong. And in the tongue of Muslims, I say to you, 'As-Salamu Alaykum'".

Afterwards, I sat at my desk for a few minutes, gathering my thoughts, awe-struck at the just-concluded conversation.

I told my editor, and the story was turned around in a matter of days, and ran the Tuesday before the march on page 10, much further back than where I thought an article of such magnitude should be placed.

Not that I thought it should have led the paper; but what further incensed me was the editor's decision not to even tease the

Farrakhan Q&A on the cover of that day's paper: no tag, no mention of it, nothing at all.

In fact, if one weren't a regular reader of the paper, it's quite possible to have missed it entirely.

Even competing local media outlets didn't pick up on the interview.

To this day, I am mystified by the lack of coverage in the Philadelphia region in regards to Farrakhan's mission.

And to some extent, that's exactly what happened, as I received zero feedback on the story.

Not one letter, e-mail or phone call, either saying how great it was or complaining about giving a world-class hatemonger such a platform (I was used to getting e-mails and correspondence like that concerning other stories I had written).

I was almost certain I would hear from at least one person representing a Jewish rights' organization, but that, too, never materialized.

In fact, the only internal response, if one can even define it as such, was during a fire alarm drill.

I was standing across the street from the paper with Editorial Cartoonist Signe Wilkerson, and she asked me how did my interview with "Louie" go. It took me a second to figure out that she was talking about Farrakhan.

I told her it was the best interview of my life. And that was the end of the feedback from the paper's rank-and-file.

I guess in the end though, that is what the editors wanted the story to be: solid, but with no controversy. Why stir up a hornet's nest?

That's just the way the Daily News rolled with this story.

While it could be said that the editors dropped the ball on the Farrakhan story, Heine and Days came down hard on me when

I didn't attend the march itself and come back with day-of material.

Apparently inconsequential to Heine and Days (Which sounds like a law firm or a bad cop, worse cop tandem) was the fact I had already done an exhaustive amount of work on the running package, including folding quotes not used in the Q&A into a story that advanced Farrakhan's appearance at a North Philly church.

I was under the impression that I was to only cover the ramp-up, and that my work was done after the Farrakhan interview and the "If You Go" sidebar that accompanied the last of the write-ups for the Millions More Movement package. And besides, for two weeks leading up to the march, I had e-mailed and asked Heine and another former dayside editor, Yvonne Dennis, if they wanted me to go.

I never received an answer, and I certainly wasn't going to take it upon myself to go, especially on my own dime. I already spoke to The Man and wrapped up the package; what more could the paper want?

A whole helluva lot more, as it turned out.

The night of the March and long after it concluded, Days called with an indignant, alarmed tone, asking "boy, where is the March story?" He approached me as if he were scorning his youngest child.

I told him that no article would be forthcoming because I didn't go. I then explained to him that for two weeks, I haven't received any feedback about assigning me to go, so I wasn't going to assume that I should.

After an awkward silence, I could tell that Days was irate, but he let the conversation go at that. As I look back though, I should have relayed to Days how salty I was that the interview didn't get any sort of front-page play the day that it ran, but that would have been a fruitless statement; everyone knows that writers write, and have little overall say-so in the packaging and placement of a story.

For good reason, I doubted that would be the end of it, and like most times when I felt impending newsroom doom from one source or another, I had trouble sleeping. Which was almost nightly.

The Monday after the March, Heine, in full red-faced editor mode, steamed towards my desk, which was located in the features department at the time, because I was still mainly a features reporter. Not too many writers at the paper were pulling that sort of double duty. Soon though, my desk would be moved to the crime team section of the newsroom, a move that would eventually lead to some other shit.

Good thing I seen him coming, because I was ready to stand toe-to-toe with him by the time he got to me.

"Why didn't you go Washington? We had you assigned for it."

Off the bat I could tell that Heine was trying to bully me, but I was already seasoned at baring my teeth with editors and peers, especially after almost coming to blows with Jon Takiff, an old-school tech writer and pop music critic who liked to throw his weight – and voice – around.

And I witnessed Heine bully younger reporters, so I made a promise to myself to not take that kind of editor heat, especially from the aloof Heine.

So I instantly prepared myself to dig in right along with Heine. No way was I going to let this dude shout me down; not on that day, not after going all-in on this piece.

"Well, I didn't go because no editor assigned me to go. I sent you e-mails all week about it. When I didn't hear back from you, I figured you didn't want me to go, so I didn't bother going."

Out of the corner of my eye, I could see former Assistant Features Editor Donna

Williams-Vance tuning in to the earlymorning duel. She had since left the paper, but we got along wonderfully, as she was like an older sister to me, or an around-the-way type of oldhead homegirl.

In fact, she was one of the "realest" folks there, black or white. Tanya Pendleton was also like that. Donna and I remain close friends to this day.

"Well, did you want us to draw you a map and make the reservations for you?" Heine quipped.

"No, but I did expect my editors to act like such and give me some kind of feedback for such a crucial assignment," I shot back, all the while staring right into his eyes.

With that, Heine stormed off, and Donna smiled at me for taking him on, and that was the end of that.

I heard nothing more about it, and no discipline was ever meted out for the Heine confrontation, nor did I suffer any sort of newsroom blowback for not going to DC.

That was the only drama I ever had with Heine, and that was the only issue when it came to putting Farrakhan in the paper.

To many of the editors and coworkers there, it must have been just another interview with another polarizing figure, but for me, it was an opportunity of a lifetime, one that, when I look back on my years at the paper, still stands the test as being one of my finest interviews.

To be the first reporter to bring Farrakhan to mainstream press (or at the very least, to the mainstream press in the Pennsylvania region) was an accomplishment unto itself; for me to be said reporter, a kid from West Philly, was pretty astonishing, at least to me, and I felt that, finally, I was making a difference as an African-American journalist.

CHAPTER TWO:

Interview with Danielle Cattier, Mother of Slain 14-year-old Ebony Dorsey, December 2007.

It was a murder that shocked regional media and residents of the entire Delaware Valley. Ebony Dorsey, a likable 14year-old African-American girl, was sexually assaulted and murdered by her mother's crack-crazed lover, Mark O'Donnell.

Everyone believed that Danielle Cattie - Ebony's mother - was complicit in her daughter's murder, especially when it came out that the night prior to Ebony's killing, Mark and Danielle spent many hours smoking crack together - all while Ebony was at Mark's apartment, baby-sitting Mark's biological child.

And to say that the editors were thirsty for blood - that of Danielle's and Mark's - would be a gross understatement, because the entire newsroom and much of the general public felt that Ebony didn't deserve such a gruesome ending to her young, innocent life.

Cops said that Mark strangled Ebony with her pajamas before sexually assaulting her with a foreign object.

That's some sick shit, made even more bizarre by Mark's incoherent ramblings to the assembled press corps and to no one in particular as he was being led from the Montgomery County District Attorney's office to an awaiting police wagon.

Mark claimed the reason he killed ebony was because he caught Ebony molesting his child when the finally returned home.

Throughout his outburst, Mark failed to reason how he could go from supposedly witnessing his daughter's assault to killing and then sexually assaulting the child's corpse.

Of course, everyone knew that Mark's prolonged crack use fueled the deadly encounter.

And it didn't help matters much that Danielle seemed distant and wasn't reacting in the manner one thinks a mother would after learning that her daughter was murdered and then sexually violatedby her lover.

After covering many a grieving parent, I have seen many shades of emotional pain, and to this day, I believe that whatever emotion Danielle displayed was merely a charade to drum up support for a grieving, drug-addicted mother.

Later on, she even went as far as to submit a lengthy op/ed - which the editorial page editor happily ran on the front page of the editorial section - in which she blamed Mark for everything that happened while conspicuously leaving out the part about hitting the pipe with a married man.

Danielle, rightly so, received an incredible amount of negative feedback, as one could imagine. I mean, what did she expect, for people to sympathize with her, beyond the point of feeling the associative sorrow of a young life lost?

After numerous visits to the Montgomery County District Attorney's office, I was tasked with finding out where Danielle lived and convincing her to talk with me. The editors approached it as a shot in the dark, basically because it happened in a relatively distant township and that even if I found out where Danielle lived, there was now way she was going to talk. Not with all the legal and public heat burning her.

Shifting through stacks of court documents and the available public records, I was able to find out where Danielle lived, and after Mark's preliminary hearing (the one in which he shocked even hardcore court reporters with his diatribe against his victim) and with the assistance of my iPhone and by almost sheer miracle, after several wrong turns and long stretches of woodsy, suburban road, I found myself outside of Danielle's rather dilapidated dwelling, which sat in the middle of an altogether depressed and bleak-looking neighborhood.

There went my belief that everything suburbs was plush and shiny.

Parked diagonally from Cattie's house in one of the paper's fleet of PT Cruiser staff cars, I remember feeling that I really didn't want to do this. But I didn't come all that way to not do it, either.

Summoning up nerve and cool, I knocked on Danielle's door, introduced myself, and asked her if she wouldn't mind speaking to me about the life of her daughter, what she was like and things of that sort.

I could tell that something was amiss in the residence, but the vibe wasn't one of mourning. It did feel like Danielle's family formed a defensive front, and they sure as hell weren't going to deal with the media.

Then again, I guess they never expected the media to show up at their front door, either.

A trick I picked up when dealing with a reluctant subject on a cold house-end was to offer sympathy and caring right out front, while immediately asking about the good side of the deceased.

The backstory of little Ebony Dorsey was one of a hard, young life, one born into instability and surrounded by drug abuse. Still, she somehow managed to retain a positive outlook on life and had many friends, both at school and in her neighborhood.

I still think of what Ebony endured during her 14 years of survival under the most deplorable of conditions.

So, when Danielle came to the door, I first told her how sorry I was for her loss, and if there was ever anything that I could do for her as a reporter, let me know. Sure, I knew going in that Danielle didn't kill her daughter, but I felt that she could have at least prevented it. And not that I lied, for I don't know how I would have reacted had she actually called for some assistance, but at this point, I was determined to get the story.

Nonetheless, I put my personal beliefs to the side and offered the olive branch, along with my card.

Danielle accepted both, and I told her that I wasn't there to talk about the case nor her relationship with Mark (which wasn't a lie; there would be other reporters later in the day that would pry into every nook and cranny of Danielle and Mark's murky relationship); rather, I wanted to talk about Ebony, what type of budding young woman she was, the things she liked and to gather any other information that Danielle would like to share.

Of course, I was sure to also get Danielle's number as soon as I could; the editors liked nothing more than when a reporter comes back to the newsroom not only with a thorough interview, but with a direct connect to the subject as well - especially someone as reluctant and in-demand as Danielle Cattie.

Ebony's father, Evan Dorsey, was a Villanova student and ⎕⎕ Danielle Cattie attended Immaculata when they met at a mixer about two decades prior to this tragedy. Later, they had a child together - Ebony Dorsey - but never married.

Police immediately confirmed that Danielle had a longstanding coke habit, but Evan apparently looked beyond that, as both Danielle and Evan supposedly shared a great love for Ebony, an honors student at Wissahickon High School, which sits in the suburbs right outside of Philly.

During our chat on her listing porch, Danielle spoke about her life and her loss, but also lashed out at her daughter's killer, calling him a monster. I stood there, silent, amazed at the script-flip Danielle just pulled.

"People need to realize, regardless of anything that has been said, Mark is the monster," Danielle said. "We've been together for four years and there was no way to tell that this was going to happen."

That's the thing about crack use, I've learned; one never can foretell the more sordid actions of someone hooked on it.

Mark, who was married to another woman when he brutally killed Ebony, told cops that he took Ebony to his apartment to baby-sit his daughter while his wife was away, and came home in the predawn hours to find her changing the child's diaper and flew into a rage and attacked her.

Mark said he thought Ebony was molesting the child - a pitiful, unfounded allegation that authorities immediately refuted.

The fact that Danielle was shacking up and coking with Mark while he was legally married to another woman somehow didn't make major newsroom news, maybe because of all the other news going on, and perhaps due to the development of other leads and details in this case.

Still, I thought that was a crucial part of that story, because it once again exposed how shallow Danielle and Mark truly were.

Mark repeatedly made those claims that he caught Ebony sexually abusing his daughter at every opportunity, and I was absolutely stunned at this creature's audacity.

Bad enough he killed Ebony; now, Mark was trying to kill her reputation in like fashion.

I remember becoming physically sick to my stomach that this man could further desecrate the memory of Ebony Dorsey. Right then, I wanted to portray him as the most despicable man to ever walk the planet, but there was enough of that sentiment to go around for Danielle as well, because we all believed her hands were just as blood-soaked.

After killing Ebony and desecrating the corpse, Mark then placed her body in a blue tub in his bedroom, and later concealed it under leaves at a relative's house.

Police found Ebony's body two days later.

The brutal details were only beginning to trickle out. According to an affidavit of probable cause, police said Danielle told them she had been snorting coke for the past several years and more frequently over the past several months leading up to Ebony's murder.

Danielle also told police that Mark converted the powdered cocaine into crack and smoked it. Apparently, Danielle was too coked up to notice Ebony's absence, because

It's telling that Danielle did not report Ebony missing until Friday night, although the girl had been absent from school that day. Crack can do that.

"There was never any reason for any of us to feel that

Ebony shouldn't live with me", Danielle told me. "Ebony was happy where she was. She didn't have any problems at the house."

I could look in Danielle's eyes and tell she was lying to me, and doing a poor job at it.

The house, from what I could tell, was utterly filthy, barely fit for human habitation. The porch, situated on a leaning foundation, was littered with old baby toys, while two crustylooking, once-white plastic chairs leaned in like fashion.

Once I peeped into the house, I saw more of the same, along with a trampled carpet and other dirty objects strewn about the hallway leading from the front door to the living room. Muted music and chatter capped off the depressing ambiance.

It looked like a trap house.

It amazed me that Ebony could flourish in such nightmare conditions; a rose sprouting through the sidewalk, indeed.

Danielle, with a straight face, said Mark's drug use had nothing to do with Ebony.

"She was just a bright star, full of life; just a happy child.

She loved school, she was very proud of her accomplishments and her grades," Danielle said, doing her best to sound like a pained parent.

Typical of such situations, Danielle said that Ebony indeed helped raise three other younger children. "But she enjoyed herself." I hardly believed that.

At length, Danielle told me that she thought the world of Evan, Ebony's father, and that he was in her life as much as he could be.

That was all she would say to me about Ebony's father.

"Evan was the picture-perfect father. He was in

constant contact with

Ebony," Danielle said to me. "Evan would pick Ebony up on weekends and bring her to his house every summer to live with him and his grandmother."

Almost simultaneously, editors back in the newsroom ordered another team of reporters to track down Evan and get comments from him. They did catch up to him, but I don't know if he provided any useful quotes.

"He may not have raised Ebony, but he was up on her school work, would get her school clothes. She would spend every summer with him."

Word had it that tragically, the last call on Ebony's cell phone was from Evan, who called her every morning to wake her for school.

"Ebony was Evan's only child. It's one thing to have a child taken, but this is unbearable. Yes, a bad decision was made, but that doesn't change the fact that I loved my daughter. Ebony lived with me all her life, outside of a period when she was two or three when she lived with Evan," Danielle said, holding back tears.

"I just miss my baby."

That was the closest Danielle came to taking any responsibility in the death of her daughter.

Leaving Danielle's steps, I had the sudden urge to cry.

Being a father of two small children myself, I was on the verge of tears both for the tender life that was lost, but out of anger at the lack of caring and parenting exhibited by Ebony's cokehead mother and her murderous lover.

Because Ebony Dorsey deserved better.

Once composed and in my car, I called my daytime news editor, Barbara Laker, and informed her of my success in not only finding Danielle Cattie, but in getting that world-exclusive interview with her as well.

At the time, all local media outlets were looking for Danielle, and so far, no member of that collective had been able to locate her. It was a coup for the paper, and really only involved a little snooping and hustle on my part.

And the reason I called from the car instead of coming back to the newsroom first was due to another lesson learned through the fires of daily reporting.

Turns out, it was much better for a reporter to call the editor from the scene with the info one gathered, because an editor could tell the reporter what other info to get or what other courses of action to take, instead of driving all the way back to the newsroom for the next set of orders.

I had once made the mistake of not calling, and City Desk Editor Yvette Ousley raked me over the coals for coming back empty handed, and after commanding me to drive all the way back out to the scene to get the required information, she suggested that I always call from the scene.

Ever since that conversation, I have always called the news desk before returning.

I could be covering a simple, fairly automatic press conference at City Hall, and I would still call. The editors grew to appreciate that extra step, and it often led to me beating other media to spot news, and currying favor with the editors was usually a good thing.

And it was a good thing that I called Barbara, because she wanted me to go back to Danielle and ask some more specific, pointed questions.

Shit.

Hardly any reporter enjoyed doing house-ends - visiting the residence of a distressed victim or relative of a victim - and asking uncomfortable questions at the worst possible time.

The only thing worse than doing it once is doing it twice.

And Barbara, a shrewd former city beat reporter with reputation nonparallel as a fearless, bulldog reporter, wanted me to ask Danielle more about her and Mark's drug use.

Gathering up the last of my reservoir of nerve, I again knocked on her door, and this time I opened up by asking if the paper could have a picture of Ebony and if she wouldn't mind answering just a few more questions.

As expected, Danielle slammed the door in my face.

Not to worry, as the resourceful photo editors at the paper were crafty enough to locate the most recent yearbook from Wissahickon High, which included a picture of a smiling, apparently happy Ebony Dorsey.

Needless to say, the editors ran with that picture.

Never before have I been so relieved to hear the bang of a slammed door and feel the echoing jar of a rattling doorframe. And with that, I called Barbara and let her know that Danielle has become hostile, and Barbara asked that I stand down until the photo team arrived.

Waiting for the photographer to arrive was excruciating.

It wasn't the anxiety of writing the piece of the excitement of corralling Danielle for the interview; no, it was excruciating because I had to find a men's room or a tree - fast.

Unfortunately, neither were available, and after a fruitless attempt to use the rest room at the locked Legion Lodge (which was located at the very end of Danielle's block), I resorted to fashioning an old Pepsi bottle into a sort of onthe-spot potty. Something told me that Danielle wouldn't invite me in to use her bathroom, and could you picture any neighbor letting me in to use the bathroom?

And hitting up a tree was out of the question for legal, logistical and visibility issues.

In the field, a reporter's gotta do what a reporter's gotta do. No, the Pepsi bottle would have to work.

Finally, the photographer showed up about an hour latter, and I filled her in on Danielle's disposition while pointing out the house.

Now, photographers roll differently than reporters, and from what I have seen, most subjects would be more willing to have their picture taken than talk to reporters. And it helps to have long-throw lenses.

I then returned to the newsroom to settle in for a long afternoon of filing, editing, more editing before finally, filing. As redundant as that appears, that was the typical story cycle.

Once back at the newsroom though, the editors, ever ready to wring as much blood out of a story as possible, wanted even more on Danielle. Where did she work? How long? Does she have any living relatives? The editors were hell-bent on beating not only the main print competition, but the broadcast news as well, which were beginning to catch up to Dorsey and others.

Still, even TV couldn't get the interview with Danielle Cattie.

As they usually do, the editors split up the story into angles, and handed veteran reporter Gloria Campisi the task of calling Danielle and seeing, once again, if she would be willing to talk. When Danielle and I first spoke, the first thing I did was get a contact number – just in case.

As I thought she would, Danielle hung up on Gloria, and that was the last time the paper ever had contact with Danielle Cattie, save for that woe-is-me editorial she wrote that Editorial Page Editor Michael Schefer decided to publish a few weeks after Ebony's death.

But the paper wasn't through with Mark, who had the charge of statutory rape added to his lengthy list of charges, on what would have been Ebony's 15th birthday.

One thing that can be said about the editors; they can absolutely shape public opinion, whether by polishing up a bright story about a neighborhood hero, or rolling in the fires of hell upon the dredges of society.

And it was of the editors' opinion that Mark was indeed a beast, a whole team of reporters where assigned to uncover every seedy element of Mark O'Donnell's past. No stone was left unturned in the search of Mark's background.

In fact, the only other time such force was dispatched was during the burst of cop killings in Philadelphia, one of which I was the lead reporter on. More on that later.

•

But while the editors and other reporters concentrated on exposing Mark O'Donnell, I felt that the memory of Ebony Dorsey was somehow being forced to the background and fading from the collective conscious of the newsroom, and by extension, the reading public.

It wasn't the first or last time I lamented the lack of the human element in the news-gathering and reporting process implemented by the editors of mainstream daily newspapers, a sentiment that often led to philosophical clashes.

Nothing close to blowouts, but rather, just a difference in approach to many of the stories I covered.

For most of my tenure, I was the only African-American male daily beat reporter at the paper, and I was young and born and raised in the city I wrote about. I had to learn how to fuse the 'hood activist with a hip-hop mentality with the unshakable city reporter that the editors wanted me to be. Not as easy as it sounds.

No one knows what ever happened to Danielle Cattie after the shock worn off and local media went on to cover the Next Big Thing; most likely, she faded back into obscurity.

Mark, on the other hand, was sentenced to life in prison, and was rightfully and roundly burned by all the media coverage, and it was unanimous: Mark O'Donnell was enshrined as the Beast of the Delaware Valley.

A shrine, too, has been erected to the memory of Ebony Dorsey. But the fact that a shrine had to be erected at all is the saddest thing.

CHAPTER THREE:

The Murder of Philadelphia Police Officer Charles Cassidy, November 2007.

While Philadelphia, like many urban metropolises, has seen its share of fatal police shootings, none has gripped the city quite like the audacious, early- morning killing of Police Sergeant Charles "Chuck" Cassidy.

On the morning that Cassidy was killed, I was driving up North Broad Street, ironically on my way to cover a plaque dedication for two officers that were killed in the line of duty.

That dedication would have been for James Duffin and John Reid, officers killed while on patrol back in the '70s.

Thanks to savvy lawyer and cagey entrepreneur James Binns and the positive synergy created via cooperation with both the police and fire commissioners, there was now a program that would place bronze plaques at the scenes where Philadelphia officers and firefighters lost their lives.

Tragically, Cassidy's name was about to be added to that list, one in which already had the names of more than 200 officers on its roster.

Around Broad and Wyoming, I noticed a flurry of cop cars speeding by, which I thought nothing of; perhaps a run-ofthe-mill neighborhood shooting or reports of someone brandishing a gun.

It didn't dawn on me until I witnessed about a dozen more squad cars swarming around the major intersection at Broad and Olney that I figured it had to be something at least mildly serious.

Still, I was thinking more along the lines of a bank robbery or some such, and none of the city editors called me from the desk to redirect me to the action. So I headed towards the plaque dedication as planned.

And at any rate, there were other reporters available that could cover any breaking drama.

The mood was surreal and eerie when I reached the dedication site in the city's East Oak Lane section.

Normally, when I arrived at a plaque dedication, it would usually be a pretty upbeat scene, with police or fire officials mingling with neighbors and retired veterans, some retelling stories of the bravery of the deceased officer or firefighter.

The fire department plaque ceremonies were more festive than the ones for the police, though, for whatever reason. But contrary to what some may think, it was hardly ever subdued the moments before a plaque dedication.

In fact, the only down moments would be when a family member or long-time partner would break down at the podium, recalling the bravery of their fallen loved one while recounting any personal interactions they might have had, and the closing scene: a walking-off Scottish bagpiper playing a fading rendition of "Taps."

Instead, I was greeting with a very sad and somber looking Bob Ballentine, who was the Fraternal Order of Police's financial secretary at the time and who, along with Police Captain James Tiano, usually arranged things with the deceased officer's family for the plaque ceremonies.

They did their jobs exceptionally well, especially Tiano - perhaps the most old-school and gentlemanlike of all the captains on the force.

He would personally visit with the family of the officer selected for the dedication, just to make sure it was okay with them and to allay any apprehensions they may have had about the program. Most of the families were elated by the prospect of a city endorsed dedication, and it was quite the sight to see a family of an officer or firefighter killed in the 1920's gather almost a century later for a dedication.

As I wondered just exactly what was going on and why there weren't many officers or officials around, Ballentine took to the podium and said that the day's plaque dedication will be cancelled because another one of their brothers have been shot in the line of duty.

Now Ballentine didn't say an officer was killed, just that one had been shot. I guessed since the site of the dedication was a public area filled with row homes and curious neighbors, Ballentine didn't want to let that out; not at a plaque ceremony and certainly not with reporters and neighbors gathering.

It is also quite possible that Ballentine himself didn't know the extent of his comrade's wounds.

Instantly I put one and one together and figured that was what the cops were up to on Broad Street. At the time, Ballentine didn't say who the officer was or what condition he was in.

With newsman skills kicking in, I went to one of the lieutenants there and asked if he could provide me with the officer's name. I didn't think he would give it to me, and certainly not at this tender juncture, but it helped that I made a few friends within the department through my straight-up coverage of the police.

The officer told me it was Charles Cassidy from the 25th district.

I immediately called Barbara Laker with a crucial scoop on what would turn out to be the story of the fall.

"Barbara, a cop's been shot, and I have his name and district," was the first thing I blurted out to Barbara when she picked up the city desk phone. I mean, Barbara didn't even have the chance to say "city desk."

At that time, Barbara and I had overcome a rough start and we began to work pretty good together. Barbara was also the only editor I would share personal, home shit with, and she seemed to genuinely care about my wellbeing.

Barbara was the only editor who cared when my grandmother was fatally ill, and she also looked out for my health, especially when I was getting really sick in the mornings.

Barbara asked what the scene was like and basically wanted to know everything that I knew. I told her I believed the cop was badly hurt, because the cops at the plaque dedication site seemed concerned.

From my vantage point, it just didn't feel like a cop had been killed that morning. I mean, it felt like a cop had been shot and that he was in bad shape, but not killed. There is a difference.

Barbara, who was working the leads from the newsroom, said that she got a tip and believed that Charles Cassidy died from his wounds, but couldn't be certain.

Of course, she was thrilled that I was on top of it and told me to hang on while she made some things happen in the newsroom.

I can tell you what was going on in the newsroom at that very moment. Barbara, after getting Charles Cassidy's name, assigned a reporter to find out where he lived and to get comments from friends and neighbors.

She would then assign a reporter to get comments from Mayor Michael Nutter and since-retired Police Commissioner Sylvester Johnson. Lastly, she would assign a reporter to stake out Cassidy's district, to see if fellow officers would talk.

That's in addition to assigning a pair of reporters to stalk the hospital where Cassidy would have been taken. And lastly, there would be a reporter assigned to get quotes from all other interested parties, including District Attorney Lynne Abraham and other city officials.

Indeed, Barbara assigned every available body to cover every aspect of this shooting.

Parked and awaiting Barbara's instructions, I thought who would be callous and foolish enough to shoot and kill a Philly officer in broad daylight, at a time when there's still plenty of bystanders about and also at a time when tinderbox- tension between the police force and inner-city residents were running extremely hot throughout the city.

Barbara called back with my directive, which was to the point: follow the story (which meant physically following the cops), and that she would send out the photo team along with some other reporters to back up the story.

In the meantime, information about the shooting began to leak out.

Charles Cassidy was shot and killed as he entered a Dunkin' Donuts while a gun-toting robber was holding up the place.

As Cassidy entered, the robber-turned-killer wheeled around and shot Cassidy once in the head, before scooping up Cassidy's gun and fleeing.

To this day, I'm amazed the killer was able to get off such a lethal shot with all the commotion going on, along with having the temerity to snatch Cassidy's gun - a dastardly deed which was caught on surveillance tape and used in court.

That Dunkin' Donuts, on Broad near 66th St., was now Ground Zero in the hunt for Cassidy's killer.

It looked like an invasion of a small country. In an instant, it went from one or two cruisers speeding up Ogontz Avenue to an armada of marked and unmarked cars flooding the entire neighborhood.

Cops raced every which way, and it was daunting task to just keep count, let alone keep up.

Barbara told me to follow the police activity and do on-thego reporting. Right then, it was on me to decide exactly which streets to hit, and which SWAT team to follow. That was harder than it sounded, because by my rough estimate, there had to be dozens of different tactical units, all spread out in different directions.

Some where masquerading as painters in work trucks; others took the far less inconspicuous route by hopping out of huge SWAT jeeps, armed to the teeth with the kind of assault weapons that cops wish will never fall in the hands of criminals.

Shock-and-Awe had visited upon Philly, and I can tell you that it was an amazing display of force, from the street to the skies above.

Numerous black-clad police and SWAT helicopters hovered close to residential rooftops, their blades and propellers causing an unmistakable rumble on the streets below.

I could see agents going from rooftop to rooftop and from landing to landing, exhaustively searching for the shooter. Teams of angry-faced, vest-adorned K-9 agents with their menacing minions stalked alleyways and abandoned houses.

The whole scene absolutely scared the shit out of

the residents.

Hell, I was scared, too. But I felt more like a wartime reporter attached to a commando unit than a non-combative native caught behind the lines.

It would be that way of thinking that helped me get through this story, and many others.

One thing for certain though; I had better bring back the story and I had damn sure better follow Barbara's orders.

Doing just that, I followed several SWAT teams as they made frantic searches of driveways and various residential dwellings looking for Cassidy's shooter. The swarm of police activity gave East Oak Lane the look of a militarized zone. Adding to the commotion were the legions of media agents, who too were fanned out in the neighborhood.

I can safely say that every local and regional media outlet had a representative in the streets or in the skies of East Oak Lane. I'm sure that pissed off the search squads even more. For them, there's nothing like tripping over a clueless reporter when a cop killer is on the loose.

And the neighbors, irritated at both the shooting and the police department's response, questioned why such a police turnout when one of their own is shot, but never such a manhunt when an average resident is shot and killed.

Of which, in Philly, there have been many.

After chasing a dozen tactical teams as they entered dozens of households, I finally caught up with Alex Alverez, one of the Daily News' ace photographers. Armed with his many long-throw lenses, Alex was up for the chase and we filled each other in on what was going on. Afterwards, I called Barbara and gave her the play-by-play up to that moment.

And it was something to behold, as armies of overly-armed officers poured out of the backs of nondescript utility vans, flipping every stone and more than a few residents during the first few hours after Cassidy's murder.

I hate to say it, but I remember thinking that Cassidy's killer had long left Philly. While I was wrong about Cassidy not dying from his wounds, I was right about this one, because come to find out, Cassidy's killer bounced to Florida soon after the shooting.

All throughout East Oak Lane, officers either cordoned off entire blocks or questioned any person that may have remotely fit some vague description of the shooter.

There were plenty of young black men getting the rough once-over by the department, and one unfortunate soul even made the front of the paper for being roused by the cops for "fitting the description" - the description being the shooter and the innocent had a similar tattoo on the hand.

Still, the cops well hell-bent on chasing down every possible lead, and one couldn't blame them. After all, Cassidy was a beloved member of the force and treated the neighborhood he patrolled with respect during his 25 years of service. Even the neighbors were outraged at the shooting, because not everyone in the 'hood has a beef with the police, and Cassidy wasn't the confrontational type. H e was a good guy, by all accounts, and neighbors - black and white - thought highly of him. It was the least his surviving fellow officers could do in his honor.

By then, it was going on 3 p.m., and I was truly fatigued by the chase; but I felt good because in some way, I was able to be the first to report on Cassidy's shooting.

I was there when the news hit several officials within the department, and I will never forget the expressions on their faces. It was under the worst of circumstances, but from a newsman's perspective, I happened to be at the right place at the right time, and my instincts served me well.

Barbara's reputation as a tough as nails writer-turnededitor did an injustice to her softer side. She knew I had a son that I needed to pick up from school, and she was also cognizant enough to realize I have been pounding the pavement all day for this story.

I called her with my run-down, which essentially boiled down to capturing the hectic hours immediately after Cassidy's shooting.

"Good job, Damon. Just stay there until Christine Olley relieves you. Then you can come back and file the story."

In the meantime, I would have to call my mom to have her pick my son up from school, since there was no way I was going to make it to Powelton Village from East Oak Lane in 20 minutes.

My mom was cool with it, though, as she often was when work interfered with me picking him up.

And as if right on cue, I disconnected with my mother only to see Christine walking up Broad Street. She, too, looked beat down and tired out. But her day was just beginning.

Christine was a young, hungry reporter, and you could || say I sort of took her under my wing, being as though she was a Temple University alum and the ties between the paper and Temple were strong at the time.

In fact, several of the editors worked as instructors while I was there; I even took editorial writing classes with renowned columnist and mentor Elmer Smith while enrolled in Temple's JPRA program.

One would think that Temple would be the only connection between a 20- something suburbanite white woman and a 30- something urbanized black man, but we often saw eye-to-eye on many things, and the editors would usually throw us out there together on big stories.

Us pairing up always reminded me of the police department back in the day, when commanders would team a young white officer with a veteran black one as they patrolled depressed neighborhoods.

Christine and I didn't mind it as much, though, and we grew a lot closer as people when her father passed away and my grandmother was dying.

As Christine and I talked, police blocked off the entire intersection, and even the Red Cross was out, distributing water to the officers and reporters that were now camped out near the top of North Broad Street.

But it was as if everyone were trying to figure out what to do next. Apparently, the police had nowhere else to search in the neighborhood, and many were now gathered at the intersection.

To this day, this has been the greatest show of police force that I have ever witnessed first hand.

After trading notes with Christine, I finally made it back to the car to head down Broad Street, back to the paper. At this time, I still didn't know the identity of the suspect, but I figured it was only a matter of time before Cassidy's killer was caught.

Still, I couldn't shake the feeling that Cassidy's killer left the neighborhood moments after the shooting. It made no sense to kill Cassidy; it made even less sense for his killer to stick around, not with that type of immediate and intense heat coming down on him.

And the department was relentless in its search.

Cops were especially tense, because Cassidy was the second officer shot in the span of 12 hours, and was the fourth Philadelphia Police Officer shot in 2007.

Not knowing the full scenario, I thought of why would a criminal kill an officer in the middle of a robbery. I theorized that Cassidy's killer didn't even know it was a cop, but just spun around and shot at the person coming in the store.

It was only when I returned to the newsroom did I learn that, while outside the store, Cassidy was informed that there was a robbery in progress. Cassidy entered the store with his hand on his service pistol, which tipped off the robber.

Frightened bystanders said that Cassidy's killer shot him as he was entering the store, and undoubtedly knew it was an officer.

Cassidy never had a chance to draw his firearm.

External video surveillance showed that Cassidy's killer, John Lewis, took Cassidy's gun on his way to aborted freedom.

Lewis had made his way to Florida, rendering the exhaustive police chase as nothing more than a superiorly armed tour de force. But all was not lost, as John Lewis was captured in a center for homeless men after another man staying there recognized him from a manhunt segment on TV and tipped off the cops.

Lewis gave up without a fight, and was extradited back to Philadelphia.

Of course, the reporters and editors all dove into Lewis' background, and dug up earth on his mother, who was a former corrections officer, and the fact that Lewis was arrested, treated for drug dependency and released a few years prior.

Some, like former Mayor John Street, used this shooting as a way to call for tougher gun laws, but no new law would have saved Cassidy's life.

And current mayor Michael Nutter jumped in on the highprofile extradition; it was borderline hilarity to see the mayor jabbering in Lewis' ear while he was cuffed, with all the pantomiming and gesticulation of a rabid wombat. I wonder what Nutter told him?

Once back in the custody of Philadelphia police, little was made of Lewis' apology for killing Cassidy, or that fact that he was cuffed using Cassidy's hardware, a time-honored tradition within the police department.

After giving Barbara and fellow news editor Gar Joseph the gist of my angle, they were both fine with it and instructed me to file my story in notes mode and hand it over to Stephanie Farr, the reporter who collected notes from all the assigned reporters and then wrote the piece.

In other words, I was told to hand my hard work off to a reporter who wasn't even at the scene.

For all my hours of hard work and sweat, for being out all day and juggling my own personal schedule to make the story happen, I was being rewarded by being told to hand off my baby.

Of course, I was pissed off about that.

But the one thing I learned in the business is that the reporter is never bigger than the story, and how I felt damn sure wouldn't trump publishing the best Cassidy story possible. So I ate that vibe, but I silently brewed about the perceived diss.

Nothing against Stephanie, but it wasn't her who was out there breaking the story, nor was it her chasing down the cops or calling contacts to get a jump on the situation. After five hours of running myself into a lather, I thought the least the editors could do was to reward my efforts by letting me be the lead writer on this story.

But since it was truly a big story that had lots of angles and it was getting late, I decided not to argue that decision. I put that on a file in the back of my mind and remembered that for future stories, however.

But that is how the Daily News operated when it came to big stories, or even stories that had more than two reporters working on it. It agitated me to no end when I would do all the reporting on the story - making the phone calls, handling the house-ends and visiting the scenes - only to have Will Bunch or someone else write it. That's just how the journalism game goes.

And this is not to ambush Will or Stephanie, as I respected them both, and I'm sure many factors came in to play when the editors decided who would be the main writer for a big piece. I just always questioned the decision of having a reporter not directly connected to the story be the main writer. Some crucial information is bound to be left out, or worse, overlooked.

And such it was when the article came out the next day.

The array of articles and follow-up pieces were exceptional, but editors decided to keep out what I had contributed, specifically about the number of black men that were being frisked, or that some of the neighbors questioned the show of force.

I guess to keep the peace and to not agitate an already volatile situation, editors decided to omit that bit of background.

True, later in the week and well on the back end of the coverage, the paper did make mention of the fact that innocent black men were rounded up. I figured later is better than never, and that wouldn't be the last time I visited West Oak Lane, a neighborhood that has enjoyed a lasting reputation as a family-friendly safe haven while fighting off neighborhood crime.

CHAPTER FOUR:
85 Rounds, One Body; July 2007.

One could say, on that very hot summer day in 2007, my reporter soul died. What started as a rather routine police-involved shooting resulted in the transformation of a tiny South Philly intersection into a post-shootout, urbanized Wild, Wild West, when police shot and killed an apparently deranged Steven Miller an estimated 85 times, cutting him down in a hellfire of bullets.

It's an estimate because it's hard to tell exactly how many rounds were fired by police on that simmering Sunday afternoon, but seven officers discharged their weapons (and many reloaded and fired again); more than 100 shell tents were placed in and around the intersection of Baily and Taney Street in South Philly.

In fact, so many placards were needed that crime scene investigators had to use tents with hand-scribbled numbers; odd indeed was the sight of a yellow tent on the ground, with '103' written on either side.

For the record, however, Miller had more than 20 bullet wounds. Which also meant that roughly one of every five shots fired by the police hit Miller; or, conversely, four of every five shots hit something else.

The call came in as they most often do (which meant the officer manning the police radio system conveyed only the barest of information) and Yvette Ousley, the Sunday nightside editor, sent me to check it out and get what I could.

I often lamented that editors sent me to the blackest and brownest neighborhoods solely due to my black face and dreadlocks, but dayside editor Barbara Laker always advised me to use everything I had to my advantage -

including similarities and familiarities with certain residents and neighborhoods.

In fact, I did and still have trouble reconciling those conflicting thoughts.

On the one hand, I wanted the paper to send me to those neighborhoods, because I believed I was the right reporter for the same exact reasons why I felt disrespected when the editors turned to me for those very same stories.

I guess it was okay for me to want to cover these communities and issues, but felt put off when I was told to cover them.

Nonetheless, I still didn't like it, and I especially didn't like it when it came to police actions.

But on the other hand, if the editors weren't going to send me, who could they send? I was the only young, black male reporter at the paper, and I guess the editors thought I was fearless enough to go into any neighborhood at any time, to cover any story.

Contrary to the editors' beliefs though, in most cases, residents treated the press - and me in particular - worse than the cops.

Some locales were so remote and unfriendly that I thought long and hard about carrying a gun on some assignments. Many black and brown residents treated me ill or contemptuously until I exhibited some form of 'hood license.

But my credentials were official, in that I was

born in South Philly and raised in West Philly's notorious "Black Bottom" neighborhood, and I knew of certain oldheads and hangouts.

That's usually all it took to gain the approval of a neighborhood cynic. One would be surprised at how being fluent in 'hood can help a reporter.

Once I received Yvette's charge, I headed out to check on the scene, arriving long after the shooting but well before the neighborhood had time to absorb and react to the gunspray.

There was an eerie silence that enveloped the tiny intersection, which lies between the 2600 and 2700 blocks of Tasker Avenue.

The enormity of the situation dawned on me the moment I arrived.

The area was cordoned off with the usual yellow police tape, and I seen a white sheet draped across a body that was slumped over the curb, leaning awkwardly on a utility pole.

It was the body of 30-year-old Kevin Miller.

Friends and neighbors didn't dispute the fact that Miller had a gun, nor that he disobeyed direct police orders to drop the pistol. Neighbors even said that Miller didn't look all the way there in his eyes, and that he must've been very high for a very long time.

While neighbors were cool with all of that, the level of firepower and the methods used by on-scene officers didn't sit well with the residents at all.

But their anger wouldn't boil over until day-after coverage, which would come on Monday for Tuesday's paper; right now, I had to make copy for Monday's edition.

Working a crime scene (which usually involved someone shooting at someone else) on Sunday was a good and bad thing. Good in that, as a working reporter, you knew that you will probably get no additional information about the shooting, aside from the bare facts from Police Public Affairs (an official liaison organ of the police department used by reporters to get official statements of facts from the department) or the homicide department, and that responding officers are instructed to not speak to the press, aside from a short, on-scene press conference given by the sergeant on scene (if there was one).

And that presser usually would omit crucial details such as the victim's name, cause of conflict and a more detailed timeline of events. And other official outlets for information were closed on Sundays.

In short, reporters knew it would generally be brief and straight work on Sunday evenings, but that the next day's follow-up story would be crucial and involved.

So, in other words, reporters working the Sunday-Monday swing shift would catch a break on Sunday and catch hell on Monday.

That went double for me, since I was one of the last reporters out on Sunday night and among the first reporters in on Monday morning.

As it were, there were already throngs of reporters on the scene, all huddled together behind the police tape, forming its own media mob. I did my usual scene survey, and made it just in time to hear the sergeant run down what had happened.

Most reporters would end it right there (having scene info and quotes from the impromptu press conference), head back to their respective newsrooms and file the story. But I could tell from the vibe of the neighbors and the tension in the air that there was more to the story.

A trick I picked up along the way is to ask the average resident what happened - but I would ask them far away from the cameras and commotion of the scene.

Sometimes, I would walk around the block and ask people about it. I guess that is one way I used my blackface to my advantage; since I did look like many of the residents I talked to, in my mind it made it easier to get information because I could relate.

And I would always tell a source straight out that I will not use their name if they objected to being sourced, and that I was just trying to find out what the hell happened.

That approach usually worked, until the news cameras would swoop in like vultures on my source, which would oftentimes run said source away.

And that is why I always thought camera news crews were among the laziest entities in the entire news-gathering business.

While I have made several friends on that side of the business, including stellar veteran cameraman Pete Kane from NBC and a number of broadcast reporters, usually, I could tell that the vast majority of news crews despised covering inner-city incidents and would usually just scoop another media rep's interview.

There have been times when I was in the middle of talking to someone, all to be momentarily blinded by the bright throw lights of news cameras and a bunch of agents thrusting microphones in my source's face.

That would almost guarantee that the source would shut up and stomp away - in effect, ruining my chance at a great story.

So with that in mind, I made a mental note on whom to speak to when I would be assigned to do the neighborhood reaction follow-up piece that I was certain Yvette was going to hand me on Monday. And sure enough, when I returned to the newsroom, the first thing Yvette did was to make sure I was freed up on Monday so I could do neighborhood followup.

Yvette was a big proponent of following stories, and she went as far as to e-mail Barbara to clear me for the assignment.

Yvette and I got along very coolly professionally, most likely because I often second-guessed her story selection and her overall preparation. No disrespect for the education beat (because I've seen the amazing work of education writers Mensa Dean and Valaria Russ), but I don't know how that beat prepares you to run the assignment desk.

·

And it didn't help that no one I spoke to in the field talked about Yvette's solid run as a reporter. Barbara Laker, her name still rings. No one talked about Yvette Ousley.

Personally, I didn't care for her much at all, especially when she purposefully saw to it to have me written up for a what turned out to be a minor transgression - 20 minutes late from a break.

This was after professing to me for many years prior that she would do all she could to look out for me, because, you know, "there aren't many black men in this industry."

If I ever encountered a race-traitor in my time as a reporter for the Philadelphia Daily News, it was Yvette Ousley. I know I shouldn't have been late and I apologized for it.

But if I were needed at that time on a Sunday night, Yvette could have simply called my cell phone. Once back in the newsroom, Yvette said she's okay with it and just to try to be back on time from then on.

I should have seen it coming.

On Tuesday, Deputy Managing Editor Wendy Warren called me, saying Yvette is bent out of shape, and we need to have a talk. Tomorrow.

Wow.

Wendy was No. 3 in the hierarchy of the paper, and she was also sort of the discipline czar and conflict mediator. If Warren is having a sit-down with you, then you know your ass is in trouble, and a reporter was a step or two away from being unemployed.

This led to another sleepless night, and I remember feeling physically worn out and depressed long before my high-noon showdown.

Now, the basement level of The Inquirer and Daily News building, where the offices of the Daily News are situated, is surrounded by many empty offices and open spaces.

If Yvette had a problem she could have aired it out in any of those rooms or spaces. Instead of doing that, Yvette lied to my face only to set me up for the Warren blindside.

I have never forgotten nor forgiven that. I told a few people at the paper of my sour feelings for Yvette, and most thought I should talk to her about it, while still others thought I should let it go and remain professional. But I had a supremely ulterior motive: I was hoping that it would get back to Yvette exactly how much I couldn't stand her.

Put it this way: When Michael Days, a black man and longtime No. 2 to Editor-In-Chief Zack Stalberg, was promoted to the Glass Office after Stalberg's departure, he didn't make any special promises to any of the black staffers.

In fact, race wasn't even on the docket when it came to Days.

Yvette, on the other hand, loved to profess her blackness, especially during my early years at the paper, when I was a clerk and she a newly-promoted editor, or how "down" she was and how she was from the neighborhood.

But on her first chance, she sold me up the river to the Powers That Be. It was all I could do to not avail Yvette of the venom I had stored up, just for her. I really should have seen her play coming, through.

Yvette's move would lead to my second chat with Wendy Warren and the second note being posted in my work file.

This, after swearing to me, black woman to black man in the same business, to always look out for me and have my back when other editors tried to come at me sideways for a story or a particular mistake.

I never forgave Yvette for what I saw as a major transgression from a traitor who told me one thing only to outright do another.

Only my professionalism stopped me from approaching Yvette in the way one would approach a liar on the streets. I took it that deep. How else to take it when your black editor swears to have your back, tells you to your face that a situation is fine, only to turn around and set me up for a sneak attack from The Man?

In some quarters, such actions would be intolerable and met with an equal and opposing force.

I can say my dealings with Yvette taught me a crucial lesson: that, in the newsroom, race doesn't matter - even if, or especially if, you're black.

At any rate, Yvette was okay with my story that was to run on Monday, and she wanted me to spend the entire day Monday out in the neighborhood for a piece to run on Tuesday.

In a way, I should be thankful that Ousley sent me back out; that is where this story began to really unfold.

Back on the scene that following Monday, I deliberately made my way through the intersection, and I noticed that the cops sprayed up many residents and businesses adjacent to the scene itself.

There were bullet fragments still lodged in the façade of many of the buildings, while one could see still more shrapnel pocks in the asphalt, the utility poles and in the sidewalk itself. Chipped concrete was everywhere.

Taking in a panoramic view, I wondered how the cops could shoot so wantonly all the while missing their intended target. As if on cue, a neighbor, with blood in her eyes, ran up on me yelling that the damn racist Daily News once again had it all wrong when it came to "police shooting niggas."

Turns out, the neighbor was actually Miller's cousin, and her loud point quickly drew a crowd of more than 15 residents, all wanting to correct what they took as a malicious and not-quite-true piece.

Luckily, I was already well equipped to handle such accusations and provocations, and had by that time perfected my side-stepping and hostility-defusing style. And I stood by my story.

I calmly explained to her that, when it comes to a police-involved shooting, reporters are obligated to report what the cops say first (in other words, reporters give the basics of the story, which usually come from police public affairs. And on Sunday, very little was forthcoming from that department), and that I was out here now, on the day after, to find out from the neighbors what really happened and to assess the impact this latest shooting had on the 'hood.

Worked like a charm.

Neighbors began opening up about the shooting, and   pretty soon, it became a collective stream of angst-filled consciousness that I had trouble keeping up with. And what neighbors said to me about the behavior of some of the officers literally made me throw up that day; and to this day, it makes me nauseous to think about it.

In fact, what neighbors said about the dereliction of duty exhibited by some of the responding cops was so infuriating, I kept it out of subsequent articles, out of concern for setting a particular tone amongst the readers. Last thing I wanted were for neighbors to read the article, become enraged and want to take on the cops in their own individual way.

Neighbors told me that Miller had been battling drug addiction for some time, but that he worked every day and had children; also that he was known by police to be mentally unstable. Neighbors also told me that Miller was brandishing a gun for some time, and was even approached by a bike cop five minutes or so before the drama truly began.

Once it did, though, residents who were sitting on their patios and children playing in adjacent streets had to literally leap for cover once the police started shooting.

One distraught neighbor told me that once it was all over, police didn't bother covering Miller's body before they started removing evidence from his house, which was located just down the block from where he was shot and killed.

She said officers stepped over Miller's bleeding body as if it were roadkill.

Miller's cousin, clearly hysterical, said she and a few of her neighbors witnessed police kicking Miller's brain matter in the gutter, and even overheard a black cop, of all people, saying, "Fuck him. I didn't know the nigger anyway."

That's the type shit, if printed in the pages of the Daily News, could lead to a race riot or more police-involved confrontations, especially in the city's South Philly and Greys Ferry sections - neighborhoods familiar with such outbreaks.

Sure, I may have gotten heat for not printing

that, but I believe it was a good call not printing the most outrageous claims, most of which couldn't be substantiated anyway. And besides, the copy editors would flag such inflammable material well before the made its way to proofing.

But what the neighbors said and the way they said it gave me pause. Here were residents of an entire neighborhood subsection, many in tears and all yelling, screaming and just altogether angry and hopeless - wanting some sort of relief, wanting to be heard, to have their perspective of Sunday's events granted equal space.

It was a sea of tear-streaked black faces crowding me, some asking why, why did this have to happen? Why did the police have to roll through here with such force and treat Miller in such a way?

I identified with their pain because I looked just like them, lived like them and, reporter or not, had to deal with many of the same social issues.

I, too, have had my negative run-ins with police, and that, coupled with my bend towards "the cause" and having a proactivist nature, made me feel their pain that much more.

And I was a member of this community; after all, I lived only a few blocks away on Fitzwater Street.

In fact, that is what made me get into journalism in the first place. I was tired of seeing my people portrayed in negative, stereotypical manners by the media, especially the press.

But instead of rallying and picketing on the outside of the building, I made a vow to become a writer and effect that change from the inside. And now that I had made it as a journalist, I was going to either give the neighbors their say or not write. I took that conviction quite seriously.

I sat with the neighbors for hours, discussing the events. I spent so much time out there that a photo team had a chance to come out and take fresh pictures of the scenes and neighbors.

Depleted, I called Barbara and told her what I had. She thought it was an engrossing story, was satisfied, and told me to come back and file the story. Before doing that, I spent a little more time with the neighbors, assuring them that I would not publish their names if they wished, and that I would do all I could to make sure their quotes were used in the proper context.

Of course, when you have to hand over your notes and clips, it becomes harder to keep that promise.

I don't quite recall who "wrote" the story, but I knew all of my work, and that of colleagues Christine Olley and Tom Schmidt were folded into a bigger story. For once, I wasn't quite so angry about that, since the copyeditors kept in my most crucial parts, the quotes of the neighbors and their communal despair.

But I have never seen such a look of group pain and helpless anger than what was on display in South Philly during that fateful day.

I felt for the police, too, especially those from the 18 th district (the majority of on-scene officers where from that Point Breeze district) that try to do good work in the community.

I got to know many of the officers, including Captain Kevin Bethel, through the several ambitious programs that department implemented to foster collaboration among the youth, older residents and the police department.

Captain Bethel participated and encouraged his subordinates to take part in the Philadelphia Mural Arts Program-sponsored "Cops & Kids" program.

So Bethel was just one of the truly good cops from the 18th, and he always made time to talk to me, under all sorts of circumstances.

Bethel was on the scene moments after Miller was shot, and I could tell by the look on his face that this was a bad situation.

Respecting him, the nature of his work and what he was trying to do, I decided against getting his attention or pulling him to the side for quotes. I thought that would be a very crass move, and the last thing I wanted was for my sideline conversation with Bethel to turn into a media circus.

Where some reporters would have smelled blood and tried to put Bethel on the spot, I noticed that the press corps didn't recognize Bethel as the district captain, so no one was trying to talk to him.

I knew Bethel would give me something if I asked, but I spent too much time building up a solid reputation with

Bethel to risk it right then.

Besides, I could always call him later with any questions I might have had.

I also considered Bethel a friend, and I didn't want to out him to the bloodthirsty media - many of whom didn't know any of the officers and weren't trying to become friends with them.

But just like that - and like even the most controversial stories - this piece too reached the end of its news cycle, and by the third or fourth day, the story of Kevin Miller became all but a brief in the news section.

And as emotionally drained as I was in covering this tragedy, I could take solace in

knowing I gave voice to a voiceless people.
My people.

CHAPTER FIVE:

Crash Survivor Heartbroken, November 2006.

I think the first time I ever cried over a story was my Fall 2006 interview with Danielle Lee, the sole survivor of a horrendous car crash that claimed the lives of three of her closest friends and forever altered her own sense of being.

That it also served as vehicle for a moment of journalistic redemption was one of the rare welcomed side effects to covering an otherwise disheartening story.

But it was truly a big story that had many angles, as most do when it comes to multiple points of interest, subjects, death and grieving families.

The local media did its usual cover of the story, but crack city desk editor Barbara Laker, always digging for the deeper story that captures more of the human element, assigned me to do the story.

She not only wanted me to talk to Lee, who amazingly survived the car crash which killed friends Conrad Green, Abdoulaye Barry and Adrian "A.J." Hughie, but Barbara also wanted me to talk to any neighbors, friends and relatives, while also paying a visit to Bartram High School, where all four attended.

All three young men had graduated Bartram shortly before their lives ended.

I absolutely hated this assignment when Barbara first □ handed it down. It was a few months after Barbara and I had a serious blow-up over my hesitation to cover an issue in the Kensington section of the city.

I was still relatively new to the news desk, and I become hesitant (and scared), after I was met with a racist reception while covering a fire in that gritty, mostly white and standoffish section of the city.

Now, here was a lesson learned.

Instead of being put off by such a reception, I should have expected it.

I learned later how to deal with such neighbors, but at that time, I was ill-prepared for such hostility. And again - no one told me what to expect and how to go about the actual task of news-gathering during my transition from the features department to the news desk.

That, I believe, is where most young journalists fail.

Not that they don't have the talent, drive or ambition to succeed in the field, it's that rarely are they given a chance to learn on the job and in the field.

There is little margin for error, and little resources for new journalists to hone their skills at workshops and the like. I can attest to the fact; college alone does not prepare one to be a journalist.

In retrospect, I should have lied when Barbara asked me if I felt a sort of way about going to cover a second sad story; but she asked me that same question before, and I told her the truth - which led to having some sort of insubordination write-up placed in my work file along with being on the business end of a stern talking-to from Wendy Warren (for the first time).

Rumor in the newsroom had it that you could basically □ piss off any editor except Wendy Warren. I unintentionally tested that theory twice during my tenure at the paper.

But as I look back, both Wendy and Barbara were right; I shouldn't have allowed the catcalls from a racist peanut gallery to deter me from becoming the best journalist I could become.

Still, I felt a little shaky after that experience, and I admittedly tried to duck such stories, which led me to dread working hard news and crime that much more.

But there was no way around going out for this story, so when Barbara hit me with this front-page worthy assignment, I had no choice but to get after it, trepidation be damned.

My first step was Bartram High School, to speak with principal Constance McAllister, who said that Abdoulye often came back to the school to help out the students.

Sadly, this wouldn't be the first time I would visit McAllister under such conditions.

The principal was nearly struck numb by this tragedy.

Trying to find the words, she almost whispered that the three deaths had a profound effect on the staff and the students that interacted with them.

Futilely, McAllister tried to hold back the deluge of tears before saying the only way she could go on was by actually coming in to work and being a pillar of strength for the rest of the school.

Right then, I wondered who, or what, would serve as the principal's rock of support.

It must pain a principal to bury any current or former students, but burying three well-liked and positive young black men seemed too much for her to bear.

Before thanking McAllister and departing her office, I asked if there were any other students that could talk about the trio, and if she would allow me to speak with some of the counselors.

McAllister told me that would be fruitless, as the trio had already graduated from the school, and that most of the students now didn't really know them. And she didn't think it to be a good idea to talk to the counselors. I agreed.

I always thought the Philadelphia School District, like most entities within the region, had a love/hate relationship with the paper. Thanks to the work of the education reporters, the paper had a pretty solid school-coverage team going on, but the district only wanted official comments to come from its headquarters, not individual principals or counselors.

But I usually got around that by promising straight coverage. One would be amazed at how effective that simple promise can be.

I hugged McAllister in the same manner that someone would hug a grieving friend.

I called Barbara to inform her of my progress, and while she was pleased with that leg, she wanted me to do what I knew was coming - and that was to visit Lee.

I'm not too sure how the paper came up with her address, but it was probably through the AutoTrack network.

In what is simultaneously quite nifty and scary as shit, AutoTrack allows a reporter or a private investigator to simply input someone's name, and the database will spit out all known addresses, aliases, phone numbers and property owned by the person.

Couple that with using the "Trick Book," which is a huge book that lists residents and their phone numbers by their respective addresses, and one could not only find the subject, but also call or visit neighbors.

Nifty and scary indeed.

I sat for several moments outside of Danielle Lee's West Philly home, contemplating on just how was I going to approach her about this story. I mean, what can one say to a person that watched her friends die in a hellish jumble of steel, glass, asphalt, speed and flesh? How can one be sensitive to her loss while getting the story? Why would she even want to talk to me?

I thought of how I would feel if I were Danielle, and it was I who lost three of my closest friends. I thought of the terrible survivor guilt she must be feeling, and the unimaginable, unshakable visions of her friends being alive and laughing at one moment, only to be dead, thrown from their car, the next.

And I decided to approach her just like that. As a friend. As someone who could relate.

I rang her doorbell, and Danielle answered, her face swollen from days of crying. To say she looked pitiful would be an insult; rather, she looked exactly how one would be expected to look, after having her whole existence yanked from under her in a nanosecond.

She looked young enough to be one of my goddaughters, and everything about her emitted pain and sorrow.

I introduced myself, and told her that I was so very sorry ☐ for her loss, and that I am here to get her story and that of her friends.

Slowly, Danielle began to talk, and I was swept up in her retelling, not asking a question until her surreal, painful stream-of-memory ended.

Danielle said that Conrad was the one wheeling the Nissan Maxima that fateful Friday night as the foursome left the King of Prussia Mall, and he, plus the other two young men, weren't wearing seatbelts. Danielle was in the front passenger seat, and said there was a little horseplay in the car.

They were talking about seeing a movie the next weekend.

"Conrad sped up, but it was so dark, he didn't see the pothole. Next thing I know, we're flying through the air," Danielle said. The Maxima hit the utility pole with such velocity, the car literally split in two.

The pole was snapped in three places.

Danielle, now covered in glass, bleeding and dazed, fought her way through the haze of exhaust and steam and managed to walk away with only a few nicks. Her most serious physical injury was a scar on the left side of her neck.

The emotional and mental scars surely ran much deeper.

Danielle said she knew Abdoulye was dead the moment she seen his contorted, mangled body twisted in the mash of the back seat.

Outside the car, several feet away laid Conrad, a pool of blood forming around his mouth. "It looked like he was trying to catch his breath."

Danielle had to pause to catch her breath or choke back tears several times. I felt myself being drawn into her world and her pain, and I felt a little bit of myself begin to cry on the inside.

I was trying to hold it in, but soon, I would be sharing tears with Danielle.

She told me that in the days following the crash, she has had trouble eating, and her final words are what broke me.

"My heart is broken and shattered. They were the best friends in the world and they always looked out for me. My life will never be the same." She then told me that she talks to them through nightly prayers, telling them how much she loved them. "God knows I loved them with all my heart." This is really, really fucked up, I thought.

I remember it was with that thought that I started crying for and with Danielle

Standing up to go, I gave her my personal cell number and told her if there was ever anything I could do as a journalist or as a friend, to please let me know. With that, I gave her another hug, and I could feel us both heaving in sobs and tears.

I cried all the way to the car.

Once inside the car, I regained my composure, only to lose it all again when I called Barbara to give her my on-location report. Never before has a story of mine felled Barbara with a moment of speechlessness.

Like a good jockey, she told me that I was doing excellent work, but a tip just came in - they found out where Adrian lived, and Barbara, of course, wanted me to zip over there and see what I could get from the family.

Before I jetted to Adrian's house, the editors wanted me to also make sure I had the right address for Danielle and that it was cool with her if the paper sent out a photographer to get snap her picture. Luckily, I was able to get that permission well before our conversation got too deep.

That was the first and only moment in my career where I felt truly spent and that I absolutely had nothing left in the tank.

Digging deep, I approached the Hughie residence, which wasn't far from the high school.

The Hughie family was in full grief mode, and I felt bad for even being there. Adrian's mother said the family of the two others killed in the crash would be flown home to their native Guinea and Jamaica for burial. The Hughie household was bathed in a somber glow; no one could find the exact words to say.

I left without getting much more than a comment or two.

This story was getting sadder by the moment; luckily for me, all that was left was the writing.

As I have been in communication with Barbara all day, I called her once again to tell her how the final leg of the story turned out. Assuring me that this was a job well done, she told me to return to the newsroom and file the story.

Truly depressed (as I was for most of my duration as a news/crime reporter), I thought of Danielle and the others during the ride back to the newsroom, and I remember being a mess at my editor's desk.

After I gave Barbara a point-by-point rundown of my day, She congratulated me on my follow-through, and reminded me that my emotional feeling could only come from properly following a touching story all the through and covering all the details of the story.

I have to hand it to Barbara; amongst many tips she passed my way, she always said that if I felt a story in my heart, then that feeling would translate into a story that the readers could feel.

She said I should always aim to feel this way for every article or story I write.

And I was feeling this story.

I poured every detail I could into this story, earnestly trying to capture all of Danielle's pain and misplaced guilt.

And for that, I was very proud of that story, but it took me a while to be able to move on. In the end, It didn't matter to me that Barbara said this was a good way to bounce back from the Kensington fiasco; it could be said that relationship between Barbara and I improved from that story on.

Still, I often think About Danielle Lee, and wonder how she has been and if she has ever recuperated from her loss.

And every time I think of what the answer most likely would be, I feel like crying all over again.

CHAPTER SIX:

Prophets of the Ghetto, June 2002.

It could have turned out so much better. It should have.

In the years before I became one of the go-to reporters for breaking news, I had made a name for myself as one of the premiere hip-hop writers covering the local underground hip-hop scene - so much so, that I was named "Hip-Hop Journalist of the Year" three years running by the organizers of the now-defunct website and culture outlet www.PhillyHipHop.com.

The site may be in a vegetative state now, but during its heyday, it did a great deal in driving local hip-hop. If you were a local trying to do something musically, then it could only help to have a presence on the website. Better still was to have a feature interview or review on it.

As with most things hip-hop, it soon led to online clashes amongst competing local rappers and their teams of hangerson. What started as harmless, online jabbering led to confrontations at several venues; owners of competing hiphop based websites would also make their presence known on the site, and would often instigate a battle, a mouse-click war of sorts, amongst sites.

Even journalists weren't immune, although I tried to stay ☐ above the fray.

And besides, you could count on one hand the number of in-the-streets hip-hop writers in the city, and I was the only one with the cachet of the Daily News backing me up.

But I knew I took it a bit too serious when I lost the 2001 award to Aine Doley, who wrote for the Philadelphia City Paper at the time.

I took that loss pretty hard, although I only started covering hip-hop in the late Spring of

2001. It didn't help that Aine had her family members politicking for votes online.

Still, I felt some sort of way, I let it become known, words were exchanged over a period of months, and before you knew it, Philly had its first beef between hip-hop writers:

Aine Doley vs. Damon C. Williams.

Like schoolkids, I can say that I didn't start it.

Things got so bad that at the 2002 awards at Silk City, a popular venue for hip-hoppers on Spring Garden street, when the award for Journalist of The Year came around, Aul Purpis, standing in the back with his crew, yelled, "there's only ONE hip-hop journalist in this city!" I could barely hear my name as it was called.

Docta Shock, a local producer and culture old-head that many folks respected, called a truce between Aine and I at an event all three of us attended a few years later.

We both apologized, admitted that shit got crazy on both our parts, hugged it out and that was that.

Aine and I became good friends over the ensuing years, and she was happy I won the other awards, as I was very happy that her marketing and promotional business took off. I can say this about Aine: she was mostly right.☐

She was right about the quality of the music some of the cats were putting out; and where I was content with simply giving light to the artists I either thought were dope or deserving, Aine was much more of a critic - and a very vocal one.

She was not afraid to let folks know that they were indeed corny, which led to her having beefs with a handful of local rappers. Towards the end of my time covering hip-hop, I more than came around to her way of thinking, and I had become much, much more critical of the culture and its contributors.

I do have Aine to thank for that, and besides, it wasn't as if she didn't have chops; In the end, it can be said we battled because we both respected each and viewed each other as main competitors.

But I most likely wouldn't have won the first of the three awards if not for the feature cover story on Philly's own supergroup in the making, the Prophets of The Ghetto - or P.O.G. for short.

Sure, Philly had it's own supergroups before P.O.G.

There was Three Times Dope, Hilltop Hustlers, Tuff Crew and to some extent, RAM Squad - but The Prophets were different in that it was eight men: emcees Aul Purpis, Fat Nice, Meat Matta and Sammy Cook, deejays Ken Cut and Dice and producers Gamez and Nipsy Russell - all friends for a very long time, that forged a

symphony that one would be hard-pressed to find on today's underground landscape in
Philly.

P.O.G. was just that good. Leave it to lawyers and the business side of the culture to fuck it all up.

Even before I received a press pass, I lived for a while in West Philly in a sort of bachelor pad; three dudes, three bedrooms, two-story row. One of my roomies was a DJ who would rave on and on about this emcee from around the way who goes by the name of Big Bob The Northstar.

Bob, I would later come to find out, was actually Aul Purpis.

Upon introduction, Bob and I hit it off well, and he told me about P.O.G. Where I thought the eight-man crew was new to the scene, they actually had been around since the mid-90's, and they already had a reputation for being one of the most skilled and polished groups to emerge from the scene.

At the time, I was just starting to warm up the idea of local hip-hop coverage to Features Editor Laurie Conrad. She still didn't trust the local music or the people that created it, but because of my enthusiasm, Conrad not only wanted the story, she wanted it to lead the features section as well.

It also helped that I handled interviews with major artists well, and that every story she assigned to me up to that point were completed with no problems.

This would result in my first-ever Feature Cover Story in the Philadelphia Daily News.

But getting there proved to be one of the most eye-opening experiences I had while covering local hip-hop.

As I got to know the members of the group, it became clear that P.O.G. was managed by a pair of lawyer types, Paul

Czech and his wife, Elisabeth Colbath; together, the pair owned YB Entertainment.

Paul was the frontman for YBE; the loud talker with the grandiose plans who liked to sit with the artists, while Lisa was the one who accompanied the crew to shows, booked them out, things of that sort.

It was a nightmare relationship for all involved, but it was also none of my business.

When I would visit Paul and Lisa's Queen's Village condo, Paul would literally have ounces of homegrown marijuana out on his coffee table, ostensibly for the enjoyment of everyone who wanted to partake. I mean, this guy even had a few plants growing out back.

So Paul would provide the means for everyone's high, and at the same time, believed he was developing some sort of street cred with his audience - P.O.G. and myself. Nothing could be further from the truth, but that would come out much later; now, though, was time to conduct the first of a number of interviews with members of P.O.G., the purpose of my visit.

We all went out the back deck, where, almost all at once, group members began talking. Imagine eight or nine men talking at the same time; the cacophony was hard to keep up with, let alone translate.

That session, and many others, lasted for a few hours, including the last round of interviews, which occurred down at the paper. And then the story came out, which included quotes from other local notables talking about the greatness of P.O.G., and the photo array was excellent.

I really wanted to make this story happen. It wasn't just to highlight hip-hop, but it also was a way to highlight West Philly and the folks who really provide a baseline to the streets, as it were. And besides, why should State Property and Freeway get all the ink?

There's much more to philly hiphop than just that.

This story was all built around the huge P.O.G. show at the Theatre of the Living Arts on South Street.

I remember being filled with pride upon seeing "P.O.G." on the marquee, occupying the headliner slot. I shared a nod and a small whispered laugh with Aul Purpis, as he rolled up looking every bit the cross between Ghostface Killa and Slick Rick - complete with sunglasses, big brim hat and duster coat on.

It was as if we did it; we were all from the same neighborhood and we all managed to use our individual talents to make the story happen - writer included.

Aul Purpis and the other members acted as though my name should have been on the marquee alongside theirs, for the article. It was truly that great of a space in time.

Unfortunately, that would turn out to be the very last article written on P.O.G. as a group, as they would break up soon thereafter, leaving splintered members to wonder, what if?

As with most members of bigger, now broken-up hip-hop crews in which members start second-guessing the business practices of the management and start infighting, members of P.O.G. started to question the motives of Paul and Lisa.

Some members, like Aul Purpis and Fat Nice, wanted more accountability from the pair; others wanted to wait things out. My perspective was that Paul and Lisa represented everything bad about hip-hop, like the stereotypical white 'managers' of soul music's yesteryear who burned the artists with bad contracts and mounds of legalese.

I was hanging around Paul and Lisa a bit more, clueless at the time to the brewing drama. But something had changed within the two, or, more likely, I was beginning to see Paul and Lisa for what they were: culture profiteers.

It first started when it went from them wanting to smoke with me to me getting the marijuana for them, like some crackhead gofer. Now, it was no secret, at least to my handful of close associates, that I was smoking pretty heavily back in those days (I heard it through the grapevine that marijuana usage was kid's play in the newsroom; some folks would do much heavier drugs, just to get through the day and stress of working for a daily newspaper), but I kept my usage under wraps of sorts; now Paul was asking me to risk that to pick him up a few dime bags.

That lasted all of one run before they accused me of shorting them ten dollars. Here you have two well-to-do lawyers, obviously with some pleasure money to spend, coming

at me for ten bucks. One thousand pennies.
Of course, I told them to fuck off and I never
again spoken with them or visited their
condo.

The second clue arrived in the days after
the story was published. Everyone liked it -
my editors, the streets/readers and the
subjects (a rare triple play) - except for Lisa.
She called with the heat usually reserved for
minions on her payroll, not for reporters who
took a chance on one of her groups.

Agitated, she wanted to know why I didn't
put

in the article that YB Entertainment
managed P.O.G.

The answer was simple: the article was
about P.O.G. and not YB Entertainment; I
wasn't going to waste valuable space by
putting that in.

It's a good thing she reached my voicemail
and not the person, because I was already fed

up with the pair, and she was due for a good tongue-lashing.

But that's Lisa. She would make a scene at different venues, oftentimes pissing off venue management and making many think twice about doing business with YB - and by extension, P.O.G. - something that undoubtedly contributed to the tension in the group.

I remember a time where Lisa's mouth led to P.O.G. being kicked off a bill; so instead of putting a few bucks in everyone's pocket, Lisa had seen to it that no one got paid.

Brilliant.

By then, though, it was too late.

The way I remember it, P.O.G. tried to distance itself from, and then altogether sever their relationship with Paul, Lisa and YB Entertainment. Now, one would think that a manager would just let a group walk, especially an underground group with little more than a cult following, but that wasn't Paul's style.

Being the ruthless lawyer he was trained to be whilst not giving a fuck about the group nor the culture, Paul decided to sue the crew for an obscene amount of money and retention of the name "P.O.G.," along with all masters, all tapes and all records, before YB would let the group go. Bloodsuckers, indeed.

This, of course, led to a major schism between members of the group, which escalated to a round of back and forth shittalking between members that were either shook by Paul's legal threat or thought he was just bluffing.

But bluffing Paul wasn't, though, because some members of the crew ultimately paid some funds to YB Entertainment. The way I get it, some are still paying to this day.

I wanted to vomit when I got wind of what was going down.

I just couldn't imagine P.O.G. breaking up while they were on the cusp of group success. But Paul and Lisa's greed knew no floor, as they also sued media giant Q102 for some breach of contract and defamation of character issue.

Justice, finally, was served, as that case was dismissed with prejudice - another way of the judge saying never to waste the court's time with such a baseless claim again.

I know two things about that. One, that it would be hard for someone to defame YB Entertainment, and two, I damn sure wasn't going to respond to any sort of call for testimony on the behalf of that pair.

Indeed, months had passed, and I received a very legallooking notice in the mail from Paul Czech, no doubt requesting my testimony. But he could have been giving me a million dollars for all I knew, because I threw the letter in the trash without opening it and without thinking twice.

But the damage had been done, especially to P.O.G.

The once-mighty crew splintered, and members formed other groups, went ahead with solo projects, entered the management game themselves or altogether left the scene.

Aul Purpis, Fat Nice And Blaak the Ninth Man formed the crew "84," while Sammy Cook also did his own thing.

At least all former members of the crew are now on speaking terms and are getting along well.

I continued covering the individual members and the formation of the new groups, but I kept out of the paper the sticky cause of the breakup and the involvement of Paul and Lisa in the dissolvent of P.O.G.

They were a crew of individuals whom I considered personal friends, as I would often cool out in Aul Purpis' backyard and burn a few blunts while discussing everything from his latest musical moves and the state of hip-hop to how the kids and respective families are doing.

And 84's "Soulville" urban retreat is still a place that I gather with the crew whenever I can.

It helps that the original members of P.O.G. have patched things up and are now cordial with one another. Still I, like most of them, think of what could have been.

I don't know much of what became of Paul Czech and Elisabeth Colbath, aside from Paul still practicing law in Philly and elsewhere.

But It's not too big to think that P.O.G. had the talents to become Philly's version of the Wu-Tang Clan; there was certainly room on the landscape for just that type of crew, and at a time when Philly hip-hop needed it the most.

CHAPTER SEVEN:

Paul Rusesabagina Speaks at the Free Library of Philadelphia, April 2006.

Even as someone with a thirst for international causes and especially for current events involving Africa and its many countries, it was still hard for me to imagine the murderous horrors of the genocidal campaign in the Republic of Rwanda that pitted native groups Tutsi and Hutu against each other.

The 1994 mass killings, sparked by the assassination of Rwandan President Juvénal Habyarimana, led to the executions of upwards of 1,000,000 Africans (because, at the end of the bloodshed, it didn't seem to matter if one were Hutu or if one were Tutsi; it really did boil down to Africans killing other Africans) in the span of a few months, and the rape, torture and mutilations of an untold thousands more innocents caught up in the mayhem.

The Rwandan War, fought years prior to Habyarimana's spectacular assassination, fueled the Tutsi-Hutu angst and ethnic tension. The time bomb that would be the killing of thousands of Tutsis and moderate Hutus was now ticking, and those that escaped the machine gun fire weren't spared the singing blade of the machete.

While I was sympathetic to the cause (as I am of Zimbabweans getting from under the thumb of dictator Robert Mugabe), I was thousands of miles away and more than a decade removed from the travesty. So in fairness, it could be said that I truly didn't grasp the significance of the genocide and its impact then and now on Rwanda.

That is, until I was assigned to cover Paul Rusesabagina's lecture at the main branch of the Free Library of Philadelphia.

And if there's anyone who had an up-close and very personal account of the genocide, it's Rusesabagina.

During the 1994 bloodletting, Rusesabagina managed two hotels, first the Sabena Hotel des Mille Collines, and later, the Hotel des Diplomates, both located in Kigali.

Rusesabagina is credited with saving exactly 1,268 lives, but he undoubtedly saved many more, as he used his influence to gain concessions from the warring factions while sparing the lives of those now holed up in his establishment.

So quite naturally, I was thrilled with the assignment. I had already made many connections within the Free Library system, and I had always enjoyed covering its wide array of speakers (thanks to being the free library beat reporter, as it were, I also had the opportunity to speak with former Secretary of

State Madeleine Albright, among others), but I had keen interest in this story.

For the editors' part, they seemed to embrace the different flavors that I would bring to the stories that I either thought of or were assigned. I would always try to connect the story with the human essence, be it coverage of the Hero Plaque Dedication program or the many projects initiated by the

Damon Williams

Philadelphia Mural Arts Program.

But from a space and manpower perspective, the editors ☐ weren't too interested in the stories that perhaps wouldn't resonate as strong with the readers as others might, so I was told to not expect much space when the story ran the next day, but I was at least promised a picture. I had not choice but to accept that deal. Well, my other option would be to not cover his appearance at all - and that wasn't really an option, either.

And that's how it was with many stories at the paper, especially towards the end of my tenure there. With budget constraints, the layoffs or buyouts of crucial staff members and the overall decline of the newspaper industry, gone were the days of daily bylines with 20 or more inches of copy, unless it was a sensational rape, murder or some other calamity involving the human condition.

And the copydesk sure wasn't going to spare such length for a story that had a chance of being overlooked by the readers. To them, it was one of those situations were it was best to cover it, but also best to not to make it big.

Still, I was excited to speak with Rusesabagina before his lecture and to have a front-row seat during it. Rusesabagina was in town to discuss his book, "No Ordinary Man," the featured work for the library's "One Book, One Philadelphia" program, which distributes the selected book throughout the public school district and free library system.

I'll never forget being swept up in Rusesabagina's retelling of the wanton massacre and his heroism. However,

Rusesabagina made certain to mention that he didn't feel like nor wanted to be received as a hero. But many folks view him just as that. I often wondered if he was haunted by the visions of seeing so many relatives and friends either mutilated or shot dead - or both.

Rusesabagina said that despite the ethnic clashes, there was a time when Tutsi and Hutus were friendly towards each other. In fact, Rusesabagina is a Hutu, while his wife, Tatiana, is a Tutsi. So he meant it when he said the native folks often intermingled and coexisted.

But that had to be long before 1990, when the rebel group Rwandan Patriotic front, supposedly primarily composed of Tutsi refugees, invaded Northern Rwanda. That led to the spread of anti-Tutsi rhetoric that culminated with the 100-day genocidal campaign.

The audience was filled mostly with high school students and members of one of the many library programs, but I had the perfect seat, in the front row, at the right of the stage. A loud, prolonged ovation erupted from the crowd when Rusesabagina was introduced, but it quickly faded to a complete silence once he took to the podium.

A single light shone down on Rusesabagina as he began to speak, and it was apparent that although this man has witnessed the most brutal methods of death and had much to say, it was hard for him to find the words. Or at least, the words to open up with.

Speaking slowly and with a strong hint of his African dialect, Rusesabagina started off with a meek introduction, before he eased into describing what everyone was there to hear.

Rusesabagina again subtly warned that he wasn't a hero, ☐ that he was in a position where he had no choice but to react the way he did, and that the people had no one else to turn to, and no where else to hide. "The refugees chose me," Rusesabagina said that afternoon.

With startling detail, Rusesabagina spoke of being awakened by the cold nozzle of a machine gun, and how he had to send his wife and kids far away from him and the bloody drama.

I can barely visualize being in his position. Holding the

Damon Williams

fates of hundreds of souls in his hand, knowing that that one false slip of the tongue or one seemingly innocuous gesture taken as a slight could led to the deaths of not only himself, but of the refugees in his hotel. He spoke of how hard it was for him to see his family go, but that decision most likely allowed him to be with his wife and kids today.

Rusesabagina's path towards becoming The Chosen One happened when 26 friends and relatives all sought shelter at his residence. When the violence got too hot for the owners of the hotel, they called up Rusesabagina to see if he would be interested in managing it. Rusesabagina agreed, and took the initial 26 refugees with him.

By Rusesabagina's account, all of Rwanda was shaken when Habyarimana's plane was blown from the sky. As the news spread, Rusesabagina's wife called him and told him to come home immediately from his job.

Solemnly, Rusesabagina said he was sure of only one ☐ thing at the time, and it was being killed. But he said he wasn't going to sit around and wait for death to visit upon him.

While others my have been struck immobile by the situation or would have rather fled at the first possibility, Rusesabagina literally stared death in the face and didn't flinch.

Most disheartening was Rusesabagina's telling of how the United Nations dissed him when he made several calls for official intervention from the world's governing and mostpowerful human rights organization.

Being an armchair political scientist, I couldn't understand why the UN wouldn't send a better-equipped peace-keeping team into the hot zone, rather than the grossly outmanned and out-gunned unit that momentarily fought the good fight.

Rusesabagina said the UN deserted him and the growing number of refugees. Amazingly, none of the refugees that stayed with Rusesabagina were hurt in any way.

Deliverance would come, no thanks to the UN. "The UN abandoned us; no one would come help us," he told the crowd.

I was impressed. Not only with Rusesabagina's speaking style, but also by being in the same room with the only man to directly save hundreds of lives during one of Africa's bloodiest conflicts. The editors, too, like how I pitched the story, and although it did run tight on space, it received good placement to go along with a color picture of Rusesabagina on the stage.

I thought it was a solid piece on perhaps the only feel-good story to come out of that grisly episode.

But no good deed goes unpunished, and there is that ☐ segment of people out there that think of Rusesabagina in terms much less glowing than hero.

He stayed in Rwanda for two years after the campaign, only to accept exile to Belgium after yet another wave of assassination attempts. He only returned briefly for the filming of the movie and has lived in Brussels ever since.

I often wondered what he thinks of that time and if he ever wonders if Rwanda will ever return to the time of his youth, an era in which neighbors would freely barter with other neighbors, and when he would sleep outside under the stars on his family farm. Sadly, those days are long behind Rusesabagina – and Rwanda.

One can only ponder if he'll ever return to Rwanda. If he never does, then Africa will have lost a shining, living example of fortitude and faith.

CHAPTER EIGHT:

Ex-Offenders' Panel: (and The Story of Kaleif Tucker), February 2007.

Certain reporters, well, good ones at least, would take an interest in a particular subject, so much so that the reporter would turn that subject into their specialized beat.

And usually, those beats or issues usually went unexplored by the general body of reporters, although editors always preached that reporters need to come up with their own stories and beats.

I had many such beats, but one of the causes I cared more about than perhaps any other (outside of social programs in the inner-city) was the rehabilitation and social reintegration of ex-offenders (most, if not all of the ex-offenders I have spoken to take being called an "ex-con" as a serious offense).

I became quite the socialist reporter, caring for and reporting on the plights of society's outcasts, its poor and its forgotten.

And besides, I could relate to the plights of the people I covered; from experience, I knew that life wasn't easy - especially if you're black and doubly so if you made a jailworthy mistake.

And when one reads a newspaper article screaming that an former felon committed yet another crime and is on his way back up state, glossed over is the fact that there are many problems leading to the outrageous recidivism rate in Philadelphia.

Many paroled or probated ex-offenders simply can't find employment or other opportunities, often leading them back into the negative lifestyle that originally landed them in prison.

So I felt energized when I was assigned to cover City Council's resolution to hire more parole officers to help ease the backlog of parolee cases; the jaded reporter in me thought that this might be just another way for members of that political body to say thcy were addressing a problem without truly rolling up their collective sleeves and initiating effective policy.

And as City Council trotted out the bulk of Philly's who'swho in ex-offender activism - including Malik Aziz, a former convict himself who, now wheelchair-bound, was one of the leaders of Men United For A better Philadelphia - and Bilal Qayyum, also a leader of MUFABP and chairman of the Father's Day Committee. Many others were in on it, but Aziz and Qayyum were the headliners.

As I approached this story, I decided to build it up by including data from the Institute For the Study of Civic Values, which showed that many ex-offenders are released into communities with the highest crime rates.

That was just one of the many problems of re-integration. It certainly didn't take a reporter's mind to conclude that putting ex-offenders in high-crime areas sans any education or trade skills will most assuredly result in disaster.

The organizers and speakers talked a grand game. Aziz, who did a multi- year bid for drug dealing, lamented the general lack of opportunities for ex-offenders, while Qayyum went large-scale, calling to task the hospitality and labor sectors for not giving folks a chance.

Even Ed Schwartz, chair of the ISCV, got in on the act, tying crime to the escalating business tax that Philly was facing at the time. Schwartz went as far as to say there could be no decrease in business taxes without a decrease in crime.

I didn't get that reasoning, but hey, it was their party; I was just covering it.

The quotes were classics. Malik's wife,
Antoinette JacksonAziz, herself an ex-
offender, framed the bleak outlook of the
rehabilitation shortcomings of the penal
system by telling me that the obstacles to
finding a productive life for her were nearly
insurmountable after her release.

Malik, not one known for toned- down
rhetoric, pinned the bulk of the necessary
reintegration work on the communities itself.

With a straight face, Malik said "the
community as a whole should have a re-entry
process that's separate from corrections. The
community is going to get the benefit or the
wrong of the person coming back home, so if
the community is empowered to reintegrate
them back into the community with housing,
drug and alcohol treatment, then the chances
of them re-offending is slim to none."

Indeed a mouthful, but there was so many
things wrong with Aziz's approach, I was

sure that he must've been talking in the heat of the moment.

The cynic in me said the inner city communities would never accept such a plea, and that Aziz's comments were more of the beat-the-chest variety.

In fact, none of the speakers and others that I have talked ☐ to provided any sort of actual plan to facilitate the burdens of the ex-offenders they spoke so passionately about.

Sadly, all of that heavy talk netted little results.

The editors were pleased that I took the extra step of including many outside voices and data in the piece; to them, it made the story that much more rich and appealing to the readers (print a graphic that shows exactly how many parolees are entering your neighborhood, and that edition is bound to generate reader interest).

I owe that technique to Barbara Laker and fellow Assignment/City Desk Editor David

Preston; they were the editors who pressed me into squeezing more information into a story, and using it to back up the facts.

And the facts bore out that these individuals and many others only wanted to talk their way out of the situation, to falsely claim that they were doing something tangible for the cause; none really planned on truly helping an ex-offender.

In fact, to me, it appeared that this collective of thinkers and concerned activists couldn't help the masses of parolees now flooding the streets.

But it was downright disheartening to later learn that they couldn't even help one.

Months after the story was printed, I still had the salty after-taste in my mouth that comes from writing an article that falsely builds up an entity, institution or person, and I was beginning to feel that way about everyone involved in the reintegration of ex-offenders.

It was the inactivity following the City Hall conflab that ☐ turned me off initially.

I was turned off even more when Qayyum & Co. had Bill Cosby speak at Community College of Philadelphia later that month.

There, Cosby lashed out at the low-income and downtrodden (I.E. the black) residents of the city, calling them to task for their own failures wile pointing his finger and denigrating many in the audience.

Cosby was in rare form, even for him. From the stage in Community College's auditorium, addressing legions of black faces, Cosby lit into the very people that came to see him.

"Your child's name is not 'nigger,' and your two-year-old child is not 'motherfucker.'"

Cosby also arrogantly called out the folks who say he picks on the poor, basically saying he couldn't give a fuck about the criticism, and that he hopes and wants the media to report it.

What kind of shit is that?

An event that was supposed to bring about unity and address the problems of recidivism turned into a lashing of the people by someone many would consider a favorite son of the city.

Cosby was certainly on a roll that day, touching on topics ranging from molestation to education, making more outrageous statements along the way - including an utterly bizarre and profane rant on incest.

Tellingly, never once did Cosby, Qayyum or Aziz mention the issues facing ex-offenders or what can realistically be done to help them. Instead, it was a parade of ex-cons on the stage, simultaneously claiming how real and deadly they were in their former lives while telling the rather young audience to stay away from that sort of negative lifestyle.

One speaker in particular really irked me.

Professed ex-crook Lance Feurtado spent nearly all his time talking up in criminal credentials, and even had the gall to talk tough to a few people in the audience that were growing tired of his rant.

It was comical to me to hear Feurtado basically embrace his past, while trying to convince the crowd to not follow the same path. It was truly a classic moment.

I really had a problem with these dudes stalking around on stage. If it weren't for my professionalism and wanting to hear what absurdity Cosby would spew next, I would have walked out as soon as these imposters took the mic.

I don't know how Qayyum did it, but he was always able to trot out Cosby, you know, "for the people." But in reality, it seemed as though all parties involved where in it chiefly for the publicity and media coverage.

But there was one chance left for that group to redeem itself.

Kalief Tucker was a Philly native that somehow got caught up in illegal activity and ended up in a prison in Florida.

Tucker read the story and sent me a very long letter, stating he would be paroled soon and desperately needed some help. He read in the stories of the work Aziz, Qayyum and others were doing, and he wanted me to put him on with them if possible.

Tucker's letter implored me to act, stating that he was out of options and didn't know what to do or where to go once released.

At that time, I was accustomed to receiving letters from ☐ inmates, because by then I had written numerous stories on the penal system and the lack of opportunity for those who were released. So many inmates thought that I was someone who would at least earnestly listen to what they had to say.

And such it was with Tucker. I wrote him back, letting him know that I would personally put him in touch with the folks I wrote about and I assured him that they would help him out.

After all, I knew these were people of honor and they would live up to their words, right? Riiiiiight.

In the end, I wish I had never wasted Tucker's time, nor the ink on the printed stories involving Aziz, Cosby and Qayyum.

We exchanged another series of letters, and as the months went by, the story faded from my immediate memory, as I was busy working on other stories in the meantime.

But Tucker and I had a chance meeting in the garage of the paper, of all places. As I was coming in from covering a bit of breaking news, Tucker was working as a deliveryman at the time and happened to be dropping something off at the paper.

We have never seen each other beforehand, but he called out my name and said that it he thought that I could only be Damon, because how many young brothers work at the paper? I was genuinely happy to see him, and I remember the look on Tucker' face; he seemed happy to just be alive, to be there, talking to me.

We exchanged cell numbers, and I assured him that I would put him in touch with the people I wrote about in my article.

I then went to work on putting Tucker in touch with Aziz I I and Qayyum, and to this very day, I'm furious with the bullshit they served me.

Or should I say, that one served me, because after the initial story ran, I never heard from Aziz again.

I called and left numerous messages with him, both on MUFABP's phone and his personal cell. That showed me the caliber of Aziz when he could easily find me for some event that his organization was involved in, yet disappear when it came time to put some action behind those heavy words.

I had even told Aziz and Qayyum that I would take it as a personal favor if they would each look out specifically for Tucker.

Aziz, through his grave lack of communication, made it quite clear that he wasn't interested in helping Tucker; Qayyum, forever the diplomat, said that I should give Tucker his cell number, and that he would work something out with him.

That "something" never materialized. Qayyum couldn't - or wouldn't - help Tucker, and I felt that I had let Tucker down in a big way.

In fact, the whole community - those that could effect change, those that could make something happen if they really, truly wanted to - failed him.

I even reached out to the director of the Philadelphia Mural Arts Program to see if she could help Tucker. I thought that might work, since MAP does a lot of work with exoffenders.

Again, I was roundly fronted on by the very people I had routinely covered.

It seemed that everyone I knew in Philadelphia were too interested in just talking shit, but not actually doing anything.

I felt hurt personally and frustrated professionally by the ⎢⎢ inactivity and lip service.

Then nor now can I find a reason why these folks simply refused to help Tucker. But most especially, I was turned off by those intimately involved in reentry that wouldn't lift a finger for Tucker.

As time went on, Tucker would call me, brimming with emotion and a sense of hopelessness, pleading with me to find one individual that would help him. Soon, I became a sort of surrogate for him, trying to show him the proper way to go about sending letters, whom to talk to, things like that.

I remember one time he called and it sounded like he'd been crying, and after we spoke, I felt like crying right along with him, because now, I was just as frustrated with the bullshit as he was.

Believe me, I was so infuriated that I was going to pen a front-page story that featured Tucker's plight and the gross negligence of the those in position to help him.

My editors were down with that, and indeed, Tucker and his plight made it to the front page, and the general feedback was that people were aghast at the "system," and how it failed a young man trying to right his life.

That article went easy on Qayyum and Aziz, though; I guess the editors, great thinkers the lot of them, didn't want to facilitate a beef between the so-called outreach community and myself.

Instead, the story took a centrist view, which captured Tucker's angst; it included juicy quotes about how Tucker had a new mouth to feed and that he was "thisclose" to going back to a more darker way of earning a living.

Tucker also tied in the rash of police shootings with the lack of opportunities for those coming home from prison.

That struck a cord with readers, many of whom agreed ⬜ with the sentiment of the story; others questioned Tucker's decision-making, which led to his prison bid in the first place, which is a fair.

Because on the flipside, it was Tucker who got involved in criminal activity. I understood all that, but it was less about what Tucker did, but more about what Tucker was trying to do now.

Tucker was pleased that his story was finally told, and the editors ate it up because it was a topic I had brainstormed, which included one hell of a human interest angle, and that I used my connections to the street, as it were, to add life to the story. I don't think any other reporter would have approached the story in the manner I did.

But I felt empty inside after that final piece. It forever illuminated a few points about Philadelphia, journalism and the nature of people. Journalists have no friends, even those folks or institutions that one covers on a regular basis.

And just as there aren't any friends, there are

also no favors - not without strings attached. And I gathered that I wasn't doing enough favors for Qayyum and Aziz to warrant them actually caring about someone not from their intimate circle.

I never again went out of my way for those involved in the story, exacting my own slice of revenge for their actions towards Tucker.

In fact, that was the last time Aziz has been mentioned under my byline.

Karma has a way of working out, however. Through a falling out with the other organizers of MUFABP, Qayyum left the organization, and it appears that organization is on its way towards oblivion.

Along the way, there was a lot of respect lost for them, ☐ and it just so happens that Tucker was able to get a job and straighten out his life.

But There are legions of parolees exiting the system everyday, and the fact that Aziz and Qayyum did nothing for Tucker proved to me, once and for all, that he was right: no one really gives a fuck about a con.

CHAPTER NINE:

The Murder of Fassara Kouyate, June 2008.

Sometimes, really bad things happen to really good people, and more often than not, I was the reporter sent to cover the fallout.

I, along with Regina Medina, Dana DiFilippo and Christine Olley, comprised the majority of the dayside "crime cubicle" of reporters, the ones usually sent out to cover blood and crime.

At the time, we had, among others, colleagues Dave Gambacorda and Dafney Tales as the night side crime reporters. Regina, I knew, wasn't one for crime coverage, but I thought that Christine would jump at the chance to cover this story.

But City Desk Editor Barbara Laker didn't bother asking the other two reporters, who appeared wholly disinterested in the idea of hitting up North Philly. In all fairness, it could have been that they were busy with some ongoing project and just couldn't free themselves to cover this story.

Of course, I thought I was assigned to cover it because the victim was black; might as well send the black reporter to the black neighborhood to cover the murder of someone black, right? But by this time, I was so accustomed to covering such drama in the inner-city community that I developed a penchant for that type of coverage; I guess Barbara saw that as well; nonetheless, off I went.

And for her part, Barbara wanted a straightforward story ⊔ on the tragic killing of West African immigrant Fassara Kouyate, who worked a number of jobs, including at a car wash in North Philly, to support his family.

Cops said that Fassara was shot and killed during a robbery at the car wash.

Barbara wanted me to start there, to speak with any of his co-workers and to find out what sort of person Fassara was. And since the editors had Fassara's address, Barbara also wanted me to stop by his house and see if any of the grieving relatives would be willing to speak to me. Which meant another house- end.

The media already covered Fassara's murder, so Barbara didn't expect much; but what I delivered certainly cemented my status as one of the go-to reporters for 'hood crime.

I saved the hardest part for last and made my way up Broad Street towards Lehigh Avenue and the Lehigh Car Wash, which sits directly on the corner of the bustling intersection.

The car wash complex is massive - it has two lanes of drive-through car wash traffic, and when I stopped by, it seemed to employ a number of African immigrants.

Moulaye Konandji, one of Fassara's coworkers at the 24hour car wash, told me he didn't deserve to die over a few bucks, and that Fassara was a good man who would never bring harm to anyone.

Moulaye's matter-of-fact mannerism struck me as kind of odd, but it could be that the wanton, random violence in Philadelphia just didn't shock anyone anymore - not even a co-worker still plying his trade in the same building where, just hours earlier, a peer was shot and killed in cold blood.

But if Moulaye's reaction was lukewarm at most, I knew there was one place where I would find brimming emotion - and that was at Fassara's Kensington neighborhood rowhome.

On the way to the Kouyate's, I thought of the senseless killing of a man who came to America from Mali in 2000, trying to support his family there. Fassara already had relatives in the states; he was killed just days after his return to the States from the Motherland.

By all accounts, the 37-year-old Fassara was a man's man.

The scene was surreal and very somber once I reached the Kouyate residence. The whole block seemed to be in mourning, and a number of people milled about the residence. All wore the unmistakable mask of pain blended with angst and despair - a look that can only be expressed by a person living in the moment of great loss.

So I approached with great caution and with an extra sense of respect.

I was particularly tactful towards people that were experiencing a profound loss, and the last thing any reporter wanted was to come off as cold and insensitive about the situation - you know, putting the story before the person.

With that in mind, I introduced myself to one of the young men on the porch, gave him my card, and asked to speak to Fassara wife. A trick I picked up was to never say the word "widow" when talking to a grieving spouse. It was just in bad taste to use that term at a scene, especially in the wake of death. And usually, the subject would respond favorably to my inquiry if I showed just the right touch.

And it worked here, as the young man, obviously in pain and reeling from Fassara's death, said his mother would be home in a few minutes. That exchange with one of the Fassara's sons proved that my approach was correct.

I stepped back and gave the group some space, trying to blend in with the surroundings as much as possible - quite hard to do for a reporter with a press pass dangling from his neck and a notebook in his hand - but that too, worked.

Now came the rough part.

Yvonne Woods-Kouyate was an image of pained dignity as she turned the corner and slowly walked up the street. I had an urge to reach out and hug her, in the way that neighbors do when consoling each other, but I refrained from such a gesture.

Instead, I waited for her to reach her door and for her son to pass off my card and my request. After several moments, Yvonne came out and said she was willing to talk about her husband.

She painted a picture of a sweet and caring man, one who not only took care of Yvonne, but also of Yvonne's children - acting as strong father figure and lone breadwinner of the family.

Yvonne, though, couldn't shake the echo of Fassara's last words that fateful morning of his death.

"Everything is going to be all right," Yvonne recalled her husband saying, just moments before what would be the last time she would see him alive.

Yvonne said that Fassara worked 12-hour days at numerous jobs, just to provide the family with all their needs and a few of their wants.

Yvonne, who's face was now tear-streaked, wondered ☐ why the robbers still shot her husband, even after he gave him the $40 that was in his pocket.

Indeed, it says something about a society gone mad when a good man's life is worth a measly forty dollars.

I, too, wondered why the robbers would still shoot him.

"He loved everyone and everyone loved him," Yvonne said pleadingly, almost yelling it out. "I don't understand why this happened."

It was then that I hugged her, and once again I felt that pang of associative pain, deep in my gut, beginning to swell, and it was all I could do to stop myself from crying right along with Yvonne.

Instead, I gathered myself and extended to her my personal cell phone number and a promise that if I were ever able to do something for her, I would. Yvonne even let me borrow a picture of Fassara to run in the paper, on the condition that I return it (which I did, personally, the very next day).

It was just bad juju to not return the picture of the deceased to the family.

Yvonne then allowed me to speak with her son, Malik, who as the oldest, was now the man of the house. In the stark contrast of life and death, I was speaking to Malik about the death of his stepfather, while Malik's own toddler was busy playing in the street, unaware of the tragedy that enveloped the entire family.

Malik seemed ready to assume his position within the family, telling me that as much as this hurts, he now must be strong for his mother and the rest of his siblings.

After I got what was needed for the story, I stuck around a little bit, again as a matter of respect. I often lamented how many reporters would just run up on a grieving family, get the barest info necessary to write the article or film the tooshort segment, all to leave in a hurry - all the while giving off a distasteful "I don't give a fuck about your loss" vibe.

No, I wanted to stick around and show the Kouyate's that I sincerely cared about their plight. Not that I wanted to assume their pain, but for some reason, I just wanted to stick around and absorb the scene.

Once back in the car, I called Barbara and gave her the update, and she was thrilled that I was able to get such a juicy human-interest story, especially when she didn't expect me to really get anything at all. Pleased, she told me to come back and file the story, and from the paper's perspective, that would be the end of that.

But on the drive back to the newsroom, I wondered what else I could do for the Kouyate's.

As a single-income family, with Fassara providing the sustenance, I knew the Kouyate's would face dire financial straits, immediately beginning with the funeral costs of burying Fassara. Then there's the lost income, which would be sizeable, considering the many hours that Fassara worked.

Then it dawned on me.

Months earlier, I wrote an article on Northeast Crime Victim Services, a city-sponsored outreach that assists victims with everything from financial assistance and rehabilitation to social services and housing aid.

In short, CVS could provide the Kouyate's with the very help that they needed.

Ironically, I wrote that story on CVS because the organizers and directors said that not many people - and certainly not the thousands of crime victims in the city - know about the service, and that funds are actually being wasted because not enough people are coming to CVS for help.

I couldn't get back to my desk fast enough to make the call.

I called the director of CVS and told him of the Kouyate's situation, and he signed on to personally assist the the family. I then called Yvonne Kouyate and told her of CVS (she, too, knew nothing about the service).

Later, she would call and write a poignant thank-you note, stating her and her family's appreciation. I still have that note, and brim with pride that I was able to do more than just write a story on Fassara Kouyate's life, family and death; using connections I made in journalism afforded me, at least on that day, the chance to go above and beyond and actually help someone besides putting ink on paper.

Right then, I instantly believed that it was every journalists' duty and obligation to help the individuals and communities they write about.

If only more journalists in this city operated that way.

CHAPTER TEN:

Staying Alive, June 2008.

Dr. Amy Goldberg should be the last person anyone wants to see. Literally.

Because being on a gurney looking up into Dr. Goldberg's alert yet soothing eyes could only mean exactly two things: that you are a hair away from death at Temple University Hospital and the best hands the hospital could provide are trying - and most likely succeeding - in saving your life.

I got to know Dr. Goldberg and her associate Scott Charles through an interesting request from Philadelphia City Councilman Frank Rizzo, Jr., of all people.

One would think that the republican Rizzo Jr., son of the late former police chief and mayoral candidate Frank Rizzo, would have little in common with a people-minded reporter sympathetic to the plight of Mumia

Abu-Jamal, but we grew to have a respectful
dialogue through our mutual appearances at
the city's various police and firefighter
memorial services.

Rizzo Jr., like his father, is all about
supporting the city's fire and police
departments. What the junior lacks that the
senior had ample supply of was the penchant
for heavyhandedness when it came to the
politics and policing of the black
neighborhoods.

2007 served as something as a midway
point of a very ☐ bloody era in Philadelphia
in which the homicide rate would rise almost
daily, and the councilman wanted to know
how much it cost to treat gunshot victims,
especially those without insurance.

In essence, Frank wanted to know how
much it was costing the city to care for the
victims. Mentioning the city's murder rate
while deftly not mentioning that young black

men make up the majority of the dead, Frank bet that the figure would be in the millions.

While Frank perhaps didn't mean it that way, I was sensitive to how it sounded.

To me, what Frank really was saying that it was bad enough that black men are killing each other, but worse is that they can't pay for their own care once they inevitably wind up in a trauma ward.

I was heated by that notion, but also intrigued.

I found out that it would be almost impossible to ascertain how many of the victims had insurance, or how many were repeat visitors to Philly's trauma bays. Still, I thought it would be an interesting look.

After all, there is no denying that young brothers were and still are killing each other at an alarming rate, and even I hated to admit to thinking that not many of them were insured.

The story quickly evolved past the financial angle, especially when I made the rounds to the area hospitals.

Armed with all sorts of heavy data provided by the Delaware Valley Healthcare Council of the Hospital and Healthsystem Association of Pennsylvania and my own generally negative perceptions of Philly hospitals, I approached several head surgeons of the city's traumacertified hospitals with my inquiry.

By that time, I had become adept at fusing hard data with ☐ the human element in my big-picture stories, and so it was with this piece, melding the data with the everyman perspective; this tactic is so thorough and goes such a long way to building a complete story that young reporters should be schooled on it before graduating college.

I have Barbara Laker to thank for that.

The data denotes one thing; what do the doctors say?

Doctor Pat Riley, the vice chair of trauma over at the Hospital of the University of Pennsylvania, was much more clinical about the situation, while Dr. Goldberg came off as much more endearing.

I would soon find out why, but early on, I could see that both doctors agreed on one principle: that they, as working surgeons, are only tasked with saving that life in front of them and must remain focused; the hospitals, I learned, in theory, anyway, doesn't put dollars in front of the care of trauma victims.

Both doctors convinced me that it would be a dangerous proposition to think of the costs accrued while trying to save the patient. For these docs, it was an oddball assertion on many fronts.

Perhaps Frank did have a point, though. From my perspective, I cared about the sheer number of young black lives lost via violence on many levels, and I did wonder how much it costs, in a dollar-and-cents sort of way.

But while I was provided some of that information, most of the doctors genuinely seemed less interested in the cost of care.

I knew it had to cost some mean coin.

After my first meeting and tour of TUH's trauma bays, I felt a brush of shame for even proposing this story structure to them. And after talking to the surgeons and actually smelling and feeling the trauma bays, I fought with the editors to reorganize the story to not lead with the money, but rather, taking the human cost approach and opening the story in that manner.

Barbara Laker, now my editor and quasi-writing coach, allowed me to take the story where I wanted it to go.

Doctor Riley was straight up about the number of trauma victims, black ones specifically, and the impact the phenomenon has on the entire healthcare system. What he lacked in warmth he more than made up for in his clinical pragmatism.

While sort of shrugging his shoulders with a mixture of resentment and reality, Dr. Riley provided me with some solid numbers when I visited him at his on-campus office.

While providing juicy quotes for the story, including the fact that doctors working in warzones in the Middle East have visited HUP to learn new ways to treat gunshot wounds, Dr. Riley didn't really provide any earth-shattering info, nor would he allow me to speak with anyone else involved in the receiving and treatment of trauma victims.

Like I said, the man was clinical.

In some ways, I can't blame Dr. Riley for being a little standoffish with the press, even a well-meaning member just trying to work.

Dr. Riley was one of the heads of the trauma section for one of the oldest and premiere hospitals in Pennsylvania. That it is attached to the University of Pennsylvania only bolstered its cache.

But most likely adding to Dr. Riley's strife is that HUP is also physically attached to the Children's Hospital of Pennsylvania as well, and sadly, many gunshot victims are young enough to be treated in both hospitals.

Mix in the overall contentious relationship with the press (as a rule, no media member is allowed on hospital property or inside its buildings for a story due to privacy laws), and that made for an altogether chilly meeting.

I thought I would have more in common with HUP.

Growing up in West Philly, I myself was treated there and at CHOP a number of times in my youth and it's still my first choice.

But the University - and HUP, by extension - seemed to embody the academic over human empathy. Not that the hospital cared less for the individual, but from my interactions with its representatives on a professional level, I just found the ideology and openness to be much different than at TUP.

Maybe that has something to do more with the hospital's respective locations than anything.

Penn's hospital is comparatively old by hospital standards and located amongst the school's medical and bio engineering buildings, tucked on that perfect perch which separates the very edge of West Philly from Center City and laterally, South Street.

Temple's hospital, on the other hand, is located on a section of Broad Street in North Philly renowned for its clubs and violence.

The hospital sits just blocks away from Broad Street and Erie Avenue, which, along with being a major traffic intersection, hosts a number of bars and clubs, which oftentimes let out at the very same time, providing the recipe for after-hour disasters.

And it doesn't take a reporter to know that all it takes is one bump, a too-long glance or a mistaken step on someone's fresh kicks for that individual to end up down the block at

TUH.

Believe it.

I have covered enough shootings and have heard about even more up around that area to know that TUH is a busy place.

The bespectacled Amy Goldberg was nothing as I expected, especially since I was still digesting the meeting I had with Dr. Riley. Right away, I could sense that she cared immensely about the lives she saved and lost.

Welcoming me into her nondescript office, I was amazed by how small it was. I had expected her office to be cavernous. She mentioned that she's barely in there, and my guess was that she spent most of her time in practice, leading a team through another life-saving effort, or in theory, teaching young surgeons how to hone those self-same lifesaving techniques.

I asked Dr. Goldberg the same questions that I asked Dr. Riley, talking about the finances involved in the care of trauma victims. I'll never forget the way she looked me dead in the eye and told me that she doesn't know how much it costs and that she wouldn't want to know. Her job is to save lives.

Now I was certain that this story was going to end up somewhere else besides where the editors initially wanted it to go. Gone forever was the notion of centering the story on financial cost; for certain, this story was going to center on the human cost instead.

No doubt about it, Dr. Goldberg and Dr. Riley have seen myriads of young black men wheeled in and clinging to life, and it's fair to say that both surgeons saved more lives then they couldn't.

But Dr. Goldberg seemed to take a keen interest in rehabilitating not only the body of the victims, but their minds and lives as well.

Maybe it was because most, if not all, of her patients are young black men; perhaps it had to do with the location of the hospital itself. Whatever the reason, Dr. Goldberg certainly wanted to do whatever she could to make sure she never sees the victims again.

That was the first of many times I would visit Dr. Goldberg. Between visits, Barbara Laker, now really in to this piece, wanted to squeeze even more of the human element into the story.

She wanted to see if I could talk to one of the patients that Dr. Goldberg saved, and see if the ordeal changed the victim's life in any way.

While it was impossible to get the proper clearance I would need to contact a patient, along with considering the gamble that said patient would actually want his or her story in the paper, I decided to take yet another route.

Back at Dr. Goldberg's, I asked if she could give me a tour of the trauma bays at the hospital and the emergency area where the ambulances offload near-death victims.

The tour of TUP's three trauma bays was a sobering experience, even for me. Everything was cold and sterile. The big room was bisected by the gurneys, and the bright room was lined with chest clamps and assorted pumps.

It opened up into a bigger bay/reception area, one in which an ambulance can back up right into the bays. I closed my eyes for a second and envisioned what the atmosphere was like when the ambulance rushes up, transporting someone who literally has seconds to live.

I initially had thoughts of doing an overnighter at the hospital, staying there for 24 hours to witness the trauma team in action, but the clearance for that would take a few weeks, at the least. No, what I had was more then enough to make the story work.

Filing the story was easy, as was setting up the photo shoots and getting everything else in order.

The story enjoyed a good bounce, and it gave a new meaning to the price of life.

Made in the USA
Middletown, DE
03 October 2022

11762629R00118